PGCE Professional Workbooks

Titles in the series:

Professional Issues in Primary Practice
ISBN: 1 903300 65 7
Price: £14

Primary ICT
ISBN: 1 903300 64 9
Price: £14

Primary English
ISBN: 1 903300 61 4
Price: £14

Primary Mathematics
ISBN: 1 903300 62 2
Price: £14

Primary Science
ISBN: 1 903300 63 0
Price: £14

Foundation Stage
ISBN: 1 903300 67 3
Price: £14

To order, please contact our distributors:

Plymbridge Distributors
Estover Road
Plymouth PL6 7PY
Tel: 01752 202301
Fax: 01752 202333
Email: orders@plymbridge.com
www.plymbridge.com

John Potter

PGCE Professional Workbook

Primary ICT

www.learningmatters.co.uk

With love and thanks to Janet, Alice and Jack.
And in memory of Paul Mason – a wonderful colleague, teacher and teacher educator.

First published in 2002 by Learning Matters Ltd.

British Library Cataloguing in Publication Data
A CIP record for this book is available from the British Library.

ISBN 1 903300 64 9

Cover design by Topics – The Creative Partnership
Project management by Deer Park Productions
Typeset by Sparks Computer Solutions Ltd – www.sparks.co.uk
Printed and bound in Great Britain by Ashford Colour Press, Gosport, Hants

Learning Matters Ltd
58 Wonford Road
Exeter EX2 4LQ
Tel: 01392 215560
Email: info@learningmatters.co.uk
www.learningmatters.co.uk

Contents

Chapter 1   General introduction

Initial teacher training

Initial teacher training is the start of a continuing process, designed to support your professional development throughout your teaching career. This book will support you in identifying strengths and areas for further development, and help you meet the Professional Standards for the award of Qualified Teacher Status (QTS) (as set out in DfES/TTA 2002). These Standards set out what a trainee teacher must know, understand and be able to do to be awarded QTS. You will find them listed on the Teacher Training Agency (TTA) website at www.canteach.gov.uk.

There are a variety of different training routes into primary teaching. This book is designed to be flexible enough to support trainees studying on a range of routes but particularly those working on employment-based, flexible, modular or part-time PGCE courses. Trainees on on full-time PGCE courses should also find it a useful resource.

Content of this book

The aim of this workbook is to provide you with a framework of activities within which you can develop as a confident user of information and communication technology (ICT) in primary teaching. Further sections will outline in detail how to use the book to analyse your needs and undertake tasks that are appropriate to your stage of development. All of the tasks have the aim of helping you to meet the Professional Standards for Qualified Teacher Status, in particular as they relate to the use of ICT in primary teaching.

As you will realise when looking through the Professional Standards for QTS, ICT is in a different position to any of the other subjects. It requires you to develop in three separate but related areas:

1 a set of skills with new technology for your professional use;
2 knowledge and understanding of ICT in the teaching of all other subjects;
3 knowledge and understanding of ICT as a discrete subject in the National Curriculum.

If this appears daunting at first, remember that all teachers, new and experienced, young and old are also learning with and about new technology. You are joining the profession at a time of profound and accelerated change brought about by the introduction of new ways of accessing and combining information. The entire teaching profession is having to negotiate these changes and see the opportunities for the children and parents with whom they work.

During the year that you gain QTS, you will have many demands placed upon you and it will be important to learn how to prioritise tasks and areas for development. ICT is no exception to this and the following section outlines how the different but related areas of ICT operate.

The personal and professional use of ICT
Broadly speaking, this area of ICT is concerned with your own personal negotiation with ICT for your own professional development needs. It will be important for you, for example, to begin to use ICT to make the task of writing assignments, plans and assessments much easier. It will be important to learn to make sound judgements about which particular ICT resources are most appropriate for which tasks (to say nothing of knowing where to go and look for them in the first place).

You will also need to develop a basic level of troubleshooting so that you are able to, for example, know what to do if you are unable to log in or unable to print. Please note that this is at a basic level only because your role is, primarily, to teach. Technical support for actual malfunctions will be well beyond your remit and covered by other para-professionals within the school setting.

As you become more aware of the Internet and its various possibilities, it will become useful for you to investigate further the various online communities for education in which teachers exchange resources and share information. As the activities at a later stage will outline, the National Grid for Learning will be a major part of your ongoing professional development beyond QTS and your induction year.

To summarise, the personal and professional use of ICT comprises:

➲ ICT in all professional writing, including planning and in assessment;
➲ ICT in locating and using resources, including for Special Educational Needs (SEN) and English as an additional language (EAL);
➲ a basic level of troubleshooting;
➲ becoming a part of an online community for education.

The relevant requirements from the Standards for QTS are contained in Section 2 on Knowledge and Understanding:

> 'Those awarded Qualified Teacher Status must demonstrate (that) ... They know how to use ICT effectively to support their wider professional role.' (DfES/TTA 2002, para 2.5)

ICT in subject teaching

This area of development is concerned with learning about the uses of ICT to support and enhance learning in every area of the curriculum. The most recent revision of the National Curriculum (DfEE, 2000a), requires that children experience aspects of each curriculum subject by means of appropriate use of ICT. *The Curriculum Guidance for the Foundation Stage* (DfEE, 2000b) allows provision for the computer in the six learning areas.

To summarise, developing ICT in subject teaching means:

➲ using ICT in curriculum subjects and in the learning areas of the Foundation Stage;
➲ evaluating ICT resources from a curriculum perspective (software, hardware, websites);
➲ making the connections between schemes and plans in ICT and other subjects.

The relevant requirements from the Standards for QTS are contained in Section 3 on Teaching:

> 'Those awarded Qualified Teacher Status must demonstrate (that) ... They use ICT effectively in their teaching.' (DfES/TTA 2002, para. 3.3.10)

ICT as a subject in its own right

This area of ICT is concerned with developing children's capability within ICT itself. ICT is a National Curriculum subject with its own programmes of study and areas of learning. It will be obvious to you that in most cases you will combine the teaching and learning of ICT with other subjects. Pure ICT, which is completely de-contextualised from all other subjects and situations in the school, is going to be an empty experience, devoid of any relevance to the children. Nevertheless, in planning for ICT you are required to have an understanding of the ways in which particular activities allow for the development of discrete ICT skills.

An example might help to illuminate the point. If you are working with a group of Year 4 children, recording scientific observations and using ICT to present your findings in a database, the ICT part of the learning intention is to reinforce the children's understanding of how a database works and what it does. The learning of the science, on the other hand, is concerned with the questions that the database allows the children to ask in order to understand the scientific concepts being investigated.

Having an awareness of ICT as a subject in its own right means:

➲ developing children's ICT concepts and skills;
➲ developing children's ability to make connections and solve problems; and
➲ understanding progression in ICT itself.

The relevant requirements from the Standards for QTS are contained in Section 2 on Knowledge and Understanding:

'Those awarded Qualified Teacher Status must demonstrate (that)... They have sufficient understanding of a range of work (in) ICT.' (DfES/TTA 2002, para. 2.1 b)

A note on the TTA ICT skills test

You will probably be aware that the TTA requires all trainees to take three separate skills tests – ICT, literacy and numeracy – in order to gain QTS. This note is simply to outline the difference between passing the ICT skills test and undertaking training in ICT generally to meet the Standards for QTS.

There is some overlap between the two, particularly with regard to the personal and professional use of ICT. However, the skills that you will develop in ICT in primary teaching overall are concerned with teaching and learning and lie beyond the scope of the ICT test. Your tutors for English, mathematics and ICT will advise on how to prepare for the skills tests and may, during the course of the year, provide additional support to help you take and pass them. However, the tests were designed and implemented by the TTA and any questions about registration, content and any difficulties should be reported directly to them. Contact details and all information relating to the skills tests can be found at the TTA website: www.canteach.gov.uk. There is also a great deal of support available for the skills tests at the TTA website and in publications such as *Passing the ICT Skills Test* (Ferrigan, 2001).

It should be noted that all the tasks described later in this book and carried out through the year will, in some way, be useful in completing the skills tests successfully. It is essential, however, to bear in mind that the ICT test is only designed to test your knowledge and skills in a very basic range of ICT for professional and administrative tasks. It does not test your capability in teaching ICT – or ICT in other subjects – to children.

Structure of this book

In order to recognise the variety of experiences and learning with which trainees start their courses, a flexible needs assessment process is an integral part of this book. You should read each theme covered in Chapter 2, which is designed to provide an introduction to each of the themes covered in the book. Each theme has a linked needs analysis and detailed guidance on using this can be found on **pages 5–8**. Completing the needs analysis for each theme will help to inform your starting point for learning. In the first instance however, you will need to decide on the best approach to adopt, in discussion with your teacher and training provider, based on the particular training route you are following.

Once you have read Chapter 2, and completed the needs analysis process, you will have a better idea of your strengths and areas for further development, and where to begin your learning for each theme in Chapters 3, 4 and 5. The activities in Chapters 3,4 and 5 are designed to help you to develop in each of the three areas outlined above, namely: the personal and professional use of ICT; ICT in subject teaching; and ICT as a subject in its own right. It is sensible to discuss your starting points for learning with your training provider and teacher before beginning any of the activities.

Once you have completed the appropriate activities in Chapters 3, 4 and 5, you may find it useful to go back to Chapter 2 and the needs analysis tables to check that you have the appropriate evidence to audit your progress against the Standards.

Whilst reading through each chapter, you will come across margin icons that represent key features of the book.

 some further reading

 an example

 a cross-reference

 an activity

Professional Standards for Qualified Teacher Status

By the end of your course, irrespective of the training route followed, you will need to demonstrate that you have met all the Standards required for the award of Qualified Teacher Status. You will be able to use the evidence gained from completing the reading and activities outlined in this book to demonstrate that you have met *some* of the Standards. However, you will also need to develop a manageable but comprehensive profiling system that enables you to track your progress against *all* the Standards. Other sources of evidence include feedback from school placements as well as from your training course.

Chapter 2 Guidance and needs assessment
➲ Introduction

Contents

This chapter is about identifying your developmental needs in ICT in primary teaching and locating your starting point for the activities in this book. Each of the themes listed in the contents closes with a table, which can be used to map your progress and track the activities you need to undertake. You will identify the ICT skills and knowledge you are bringing with you into the profession already and use the tables to see which activities in which themes are most appropriate to you.

Beginning to think about your background with ICT

Before attempting to locate your stage of development in the various themes, it will be useful to consider the following questions in turn, and reflect on how the answers to each of them may or may not move your development forward:

➲ Have you worked with ICT already in a different setting?
➲ Have you worked with children already in a different setting?
➲ Have you heard the children 'know more' than you do about computers and ICT?

Have you worked with ICT already in a different setting?
If your background has been in office work or a first degree which has involved regular use of one or more of the common ICT tools, your line of development will be different from someone who has had little recent experience. The common office tools for the purposes of this discussion are:

➲ word processor;
➲ Web browser;
➲ email;
➲ database;
➲ spreadsheet;
➲ presentation.

If you are used to employing these common tools already, the Personal and Professional use of ICT strand of development will be easier for you. You may, for example, have already realised the possibilities for reducing workload through the use of planning templates. Additionally, if you are used to searching the Internet, you may already know how the World Wide Web can be used to search for reference sources beyond the classroom. If you have been regularly sending and receiving emails at work or on a previous course you will know how email could put you in touch with colleagues and children in classrooms all over the world.

Furthermore, if you are already a competent user of office tools such as those shown above, you will have much to contribute in supporting less experienced colleagues in the use of these tools. As you review your own knowledge and develop ways of passing it on, you will also begin to explore how you might communicate with children and other adults in school about these software types.

On the other hand, while you are a competent user of software for your own purposes, you will still need to develop an understanding of the ways in which children work with ICT in the primary school in the various subject areas. You will, for example, need to become acquainted with primary school versions of office software. Knowing how to create a company spreadsheet is a different skill from being able to take children through the concepts of entering a formula for the first time. Similarly, for working with younger children, knowing how to publish a company brochure is a different order of skill from knowing how to take children through their first experiences of placing an image in a piece of text.

Have you worked with children already in a different role?

If your background has been as a classroom assistant or other childcare worker, your development needs in terms of seeing the possibilities for ICT in subject teaching may be different. You may already have seen excellent examples of children working in classrooms with ICT. You may already have an understanding of the needs of young children in terms of learning generally. You will have much to offer colleagues in the way of support for how to communicate with children. You will have a greater understanding of the 'world picture' of the primary school. If your colleagues appear to know more than you do about the use of word processors and the Internet, you know more than they do about how children think and learn. You can support each other to develop each others' skills.

Have you heard that children 'know more' than you do about computers and ICT?

One of the great truisms stated in schools is that nowadays, children 'know more' about computers and ICT than the adults who teach them. There is a certain element of truth in this. Children who have been using computers regularly through their school career and who may also have access to computers at home will appear to be highly competent. Some teachers find this a threatening situation and feel that, in some way, their authority may become undermined.

However, whilst children in some settings and in some situations know more about how to log in at their school network, find files and websites and use email, they need you to provide the curriculum contexts for them. They still need a teacher who understands the potential of ICT and who plans for its use in order to develop their subject knowledge and skills in a range of curriculum settings. The children may know more of the surface features of ICT use, but the teacher has all the teaching and learning intentions in mind through focused planning and the delivery of the subject through the various media that ICT can provide. It is important to remember this, and to develop a way of working with children that is not threatened by their apparent superiority with the tools of ICT. You need to develop a way of learning alongside such children, which values their expertise, and at the same time shapes and provides challenging and exciting contexts in which to employ those skills. You can do this while you catch up with them!

The three areas of development for ICT

As discussed previously, everyone will join the process to gain QTS at different points, with differing levels of skills and experience. Whatever level you are at the beginning of the training process, this book is designed to present you with a means of developing skills and meeting the Standards in the use of ICT in primary teaching in three main areas, namely:

1 the professional use of ICT (see the QTS Standards 2002, para 2.5);
2 ICT in other subjects (see the QTS Standards 2002, para. 3.3.10); and
3 ICT as a subject in its own right (see the QTS Standards 2002, para. 2.1 b).

In relation to each of these areas, themes in this book are grouped as shown below.

Area of development	Themes
Personal and professional use of ICT (see the QTS Standards 2002, para 2.5)	ICT in planning and assessment
	ICT in locating and using resources
	Routine maintenance and connecting external equipment
	Becoming part of an online community for education
ICT in subject teaching (see the QTS Standards 2002, para. 3.3.10)	Using ICT in curriculum subjects and in the Foundation Stage learning areas
	Evaluating ICT resources
	Making the connections between subject schemes and plans
ICT as a subject in its own right (see the QTS Standards 2002, para. 2.1 b)	Progression, continuity and issues of assessment in ICT
	Developing children's ICT concepts and skills
	Developing children's ability to make connections and solve problems

The areas for development for ICT are closely related and at any time you could be working on more than one of them. For example, as you learn how to use templates in planning and assessment (personal and professional use of ICT), you may also consider using them to create a bespoke subject resource (ICT in subject teaching). You may then ask the children to save their own work and/or devise their own templates for activities, using higher order ICT skills (ICT as a subject in its own right).

Getting started, developing your skills, extending your skills

You may well find that your training and development needs in each of these areas are quite different and, more than likely, dependent on what you bring to the classroom in the first place. For this reason, each of the themes has tasks and activities at three different stages of development:

1 Getting Started;
2 Developing your Skills; and
3 Extending your Skills.

For example, you may find that you are at the second stage – Developing your Skills – in the professional use of ICT. In terms of ICT in subject teaching you may find that you are at the Getting Started stage. ICT as a subject in its own right could also see you at the stage of Developing your Skills.

In order to decide which of these stages you are at and with which activities you need to begin, you will need to look back at your experiences with ICT in all settings. More than one of these areas may apply to you:

➲ use of ICT in a previous academic setting (school, FE, HE);
➲ use of ICT in previous work experience;
➲ use of ICT in school with children;
➲ use of ICT with children of your own; and
➲ use of ICT in taught sessions in college.

How to use the needs analysis tables

After the description of each theme, there is a table that allows you to make a judgement about your needs. For each table, look at the statements in the left hand column. Decide whether you match the pen portrait of skills and knowledge. Provide a date and evidence for your own records of having completed that particular element. If you find that any of the rows have no evidence in them, then you should go to the activity shown at the bottom of the column. If you have completed all of those elements, then that activity is not appropriate for you.

Below is an example with some evidence filled in.

Example needs analysis table

Theme: ICT in planning and assessment
Area of development: personal and professional use of ICT
Link to QTS Standards: QTS Standards 2002, para 2.5

Getting Started	Date/Evidence	Developing Skills	Date/Evidence	Extending Skills	Date/Evidence
I am confident at opening a word processing file and saving it.	*I use a word processor at home e.g letter written 21.5.02*	I know how to make a word processor file with tables and images in it.		I know how to download reports and graphs from websites and use them in my work.	
I can find a file that I have made and rename it without opening it.	*I manage the files on my computer. Re-editing letter of 21.5.02*	I know how to save a file I have made with a particular planning format on it as a template so that I can use it again without retyping.		I know how to present information for parents and other audiences, which I have obtained from education sites.	
I can make folders for my work with appropriate names on them and I can put files that I have created in them.	*I save all letters at home by date in my own folder. 21.5.02*	I know how to copy and paste work from one file to another to reduce the amount of time I spend repeating tasks.		I make use of a wide range of performance data, gleaned from OFSTED and DfES in my work.	
I can move files between folders and from one computer to another.	*I sometimes start letters on the computer in the library and then bring it home on disk. 21.5.02*	I know how to set out a form for recording and assessing and reporting to parents.		I am confident at using word processing in conjunction with all other common software types, including Web and email software.	
*If one or more of these is not yet ticked, you may find it helpful to complete the activities in 'Getting Started' on **pages 45–46**.*		*If one or more of these is not yet ticked, you may find it helpful to complete the activities in 'Developing your Skills' on **pages 77–80**.*		*If one or more of these is not yet ticked, you may find it helpful to complete the activities in 'Extending your Skills' on **pages 113–114**.*	

In this case, a trainee has audited himself on the theme of ICT in planning and assessment, within the personal and professional use of ICT group. He has found that he needs to start at the level of Developing Skills because he is confident of the basics of opening word processing documents, saving them and finding them again. He is not sure about how to create templates for planning grids.

Assessing your needs

In the sections that follow, read each of the descriptions of the themes and then complete the needs analysis process. Remember at each point, if possible, to discuss your training needs with your tutor, class teacher-mentor and/or a colleague.

Chapter 2   ICT in Planning and Assessment

The theme of ICT in planning and assessment is central to the personal and professional use of ICT. The use of ICT in personal administration is widely recognised in schools now and many senior managers, sometimes all teachers, are provided with laptop computers. Teachers who are confident users of ICT use computers to reduce their personal workload for routine tasks. With the wider access to training through the NOF schemes (see **pages 12–13**) teachers have also been shown how to work with tables and templates as well as how to gather resources from the Internet and work with them in a word processing package.

The needs assessment for this theme takes you through basic file management and getting started with using word processors. It carries on through working with and managing a range of ICT resources, including those from the Internet.

File management and your use of the computer in planning and assessment

File management is a key skill in ICT. In many ways it is at the heart of everything else. When you are using ICT regularly to support your planning and assessment, knowing the location of your work and how to arrange how you save things is as important, if not more important, than understanding how to use a particular piece of software. If you need to know how to perform a function in a piece of software with which you are unfamiliar there is often an abundance of help available onscreen. Failing that, some simple trial and error, or systematic exploration of the menu choices will lead you in the right direction.

If, on the other hand, you don't know where you have stored your notes, images, music or video, you can't do anything with them. If you save your work in any folder (or in no folders, just straight to the hard disk of your computer) with any file name that occurs to you at the time, you run the risk of never seeing it again. Most computers on all computer platforms have some facility for finding files and this may help. On a regular basis, searching for work in this way becomes wearisome and ineffective. If you need an image to go in a piece of work, stopping to look for it wastes time. It is far better to know where you are putting things on the computer at the time you create them. Failing that, writing, pictures, video and then filing them at the end of your work is just as good.

In order to take full advantage of the ways in which ICT can simplify your administration of planning and assessment tasks, you first need to become organised in your file management.

Word processing

The theme of ICT in planning and assessment moves on to consider the wider use of the facilities of word processors. Activities in this theme in Developing Skills include importing images and working with templates.

Using a word processor as a teacher involves rehearsing many of the skills that you will need to pass on to children. Some of these are undoubtedly at the mundane level of technical skill, i.e. knowing which keys to press and which items to choose from the menus. Others are at the more sophisticated level of designing attractive pieces of word-processed text, which take account of the needs of the audience. You may be writing for parents or for children and there are ways of adapting the text using the features of the word processor to enable you to do this. Working with images and text is one way of learning how to address the needs of your audience. At the school level, for example, some of the reasons why you may want to insert images in word-processed text include the following:

◐ you may want to paste a school logo or graphic onto a letter home to parents;
◐ you may want to include some clipart in a newsletter about the work that term; and
◐ you may want to learn about how to do it because you are taking a Year 3 class through the process the next day!

Most word processors include the facility to draw tables of various kinds. As for images, a certain amount of trial and error is required in order to discover exactly how the facility works. They have a similar range of purposes in the school setting. The tables you insert can be formatted in a variety of attractive ways and can even be set up so that the borders don't show at all. Some purposes for which you may require tables include:

◐ ticksheets and rotas of different kinds on teaching placement;
◐ timetables of a day, a week, a month, a half term or more;
◐ planning pro formas containing elements specified by your college or school in support of gaining QTS standards for planning; and
◐ assessment sheets of various kinds specified by your college or school in support of gaining QTS Standards for assessment.

Perhaps your college or school has provided you with ready-made formats and encouraged you to adjust the spacing to suit your needs. Either way, gaining familiarity with tables and table manipulation will be extremely valuable to you as a teacher.

Another key concept addressed in the activities, alongside tables and images is the concept of the template. If you use the same format for planning over and over again, consider the use of a template. If you are having to clear the tables and boxes in your planning format each time you make a new file, you are not using the computer in the most effective way to support you.

Here are some circumstances under which you may want to use templates:

◐ creating files you use again and again, e.g planning pro formas, weekly forecasts, timetables, ticksheets, rotas etc; and
◐ creating onscreen activities for children in word processors (see also activities in Developing Skills **pages 97–98**).

Remember that these activities refer to your own professional use of ICT. Although there is some overlap, there will be different considerations when you are working with children in these areas, within the various schemes and strategies of the National Curriculum.

Making use of data from 'official' websites

Another strand of professional use of ICT in planning and assessment is in utilising the resources provided on the Internet in the National Grid for Learning (NGfL). The original purpose of the NGfL was to provide all those engaged with education in the UK with a site on the Internet that gathered together resources, which were in some way validated and useful. Apart from classroom resources and further links outside government, there are a series of sites that provide links to government data about schools and guidance on issues of policy and practice. These sites are detailed in the background to the relevant activities in the Extending your Skills section of this book (see **pages 113–114**). The activities require skills in accessing and downloading relevant information and build on work that has been done before.

Assessing your needs

Use the table below to determine your starting point in the activities linked to this theme in Chapters 3, 4 and 5. They refer, as you will see, to skills from the very basics of starting with word processing and file management, through to the use of various features in word processing, and beyond into research on the Internet. As soon as you have determined a starting point, go to the relevant chapter, read the background and make a start.

Remember, wherever possible, to discuss your developmental needs with a colleague, college tutor or class teacher-mentor.

Needs analysis table A

Theme: ICT in planning and assessment
Area of development: personal and professional use of ICT
Link to QTS Standards: QTS Standards 2002, para 2.5

Getting Started	Date/Evidence	Developing Skills	Date/Evidence	Extending Skills	Date/Evidence
I am confident at opening a word processing file and saving it.		I know how to make a word processor file with tables and images in it.		I know how to download reports and graphs from websites and use them in my work.	
I can find a file that I have made and rename it without opening it.		I know how to save a file I have made with a particular planning format on it as a template so that I can use it again without retyping.		I know how to present information for parents and other audiences, which I have obtained from education sites.	
I can make folders for my work with appropriate names on them and I can put files that I have created in them.		I know how to copy and paste work from one file to another to reduce the amount of time I spend repeating tasks.		I make use of a wide range of performance data, gleaned from OFSTED and DfES in my work.	
I can move files between folders and from one computer to another.		I know how to set out a form for recording and assessing and reporting to parents.		I am confident at using word processing in conjunction with all other common software types, including Web and email software.	
*If one or more of these is not yet ticked, you may find it helpful to complete the activities in 'Getting Started' on **pages 45–48**.*		*If one or more of these is not yet ticked, you may find it helpful to complete the activities in 'Developing your Skills' on **pages 77–80**.*		*If one or more of these is not yet ticked, you may find it helpful to complete the activities in 'Extending your Skills' on **pages 113–114**.*	

Chapter 2

ICT in locating and using resources

This theme, within the overall area of personal and professional use of ICT, is concerned with developing an awareness of the range of hardware, software and websites available to support you in your teaching. It aims to give you some benchmarks against which to judge levels and quality of provision for ICT in schools.

ICT resources in school are taken to mean any or all of the following:

- ➲ computers;
- ➲ printers;
- ➲ network connections;
- ➲ Internet connections;
- ➲ scanners;
- ➲ digital cameras;
- ➲ video cameras;
- ➲ interactive whiteboards;
- ➲ projectors.

It also includes items which are not necessarily computer related such as video recorders, DVD players, CD players, tape recorders, MiniDisc recorders and so on.

The activities in the Getting Started chapter require you to take a look at the level of provision in a school. You could audit the provision, which your validating college or other training provider offers you. This would, however, be of limited use. If you are attached to a university or college, the type of provision may be quite different to a local school, perhaps 'piggy-backed' onto a wider university network. If you are with a training provider with strong Local Education Authority (LEA) links, you may be attending sessions in a training room at a teachers centre. If you are in an area that is near a City Learning Centre, you may be having off-site training in ICT there. All of these types of provision are quite different from the situation in school in which you will have to operate once you are qualified. Furthermore, knowing about what is available in the school in which you are learning about teaching, makes it far more likely that you will be in a position to use it and to acquire more quickly the necessary experience in ICT in other subjects as well as a subject in its own right.

You will learn, from reading the background to the relevant activity in the Getting Started chapter (see **pages 49–52**), that provision is not uniformly good throughout the country but that the government's National Grid for Learning has had a major impact in many areas.

Talking to people concerned with managing ICT in the school setting

In order to extend your understanding further, activities in the Developing your Skills section will require you to look a little more deeply at the management of the ICT resources and talk to ICT co-ordinators (where such people exist). You will also need to know a little about the context of the skill levels of your colleagues and any training that they may have received in the use of ICT.

Regarding training, the government has provided, as part of the overall NGfL 'project', a scheme for all teachers funded by the New Opportunities Fund (NOF), the ultimate source of which is lottery money. As is often the case, the best source of information on this is the Internet. There is a website at www.nof.org.uk/ict which explains the current situation and provides useful information about the training so that you know what to expect.

OFSTED has also reported on the NOF funded training (see the OFSTED website www.ofsted.gov.uk). The TTA is also involved and has provided a list of quality assurance statements, including around the following issues:

➲ school senior management support is vital;
➲ training should be integrated into the school development programme;
➲ proper evaluation should take place.

NOF training is provided for every teacher and is focused on the use of ICT in subject teaching. Schools have to sign up for their training and provide a plan in order to access the funding.

The use of ICT in supporting children with Special Educational Needs or with English as an additional language

Extending your knowledge of ICT resources further still means investigating specialised provision for children with Special Educational Needs and/or English as an additional language.

As a trainee teacher you need to be aware of the contribution of ICT in the area of SEN. You may find yourself in a school in an LEA which is fully inclusive. Schools in such authorities have integrated children with all but the most severe special educational needs into their classrooms. Often, additional support is provided in the form of learning support assistants, sometimes part-time and sometimes full-time. You will find that, whatever the level of support, you will need detailed knowledge of the child's needs and of any additional equipment necessary to support them, including ICT.

Children for whom English is an additional language may also be supported by the targeted use of ICT. In this case, depending on the stage of English learning, we are working with children who are sophisticated learners capable of switching between languages and processing information at a high level.

ICT offers many benefits to young learners in the primary classroom who are learning and using English as an additional language. The computer brings many audio and video resources across the curriculum within reach. Children who are learning English at the earliest stages can access parts of the curriculum by means of such media.

There is further discussion about the targeted use of ICT resources in the background to the activities in the Extending your Skills section (see **pages 115–117**)

Assessing your needs

Use the table below to determine your starting point in the activities linked to this theme in Chapters 3, 4 and 5. As soon as you have determined a starting point, go to the relevant chapter, read the background and make a start.

Remember, wherever possible, to discuss your developmental needs with a colleague, college tutor or class teacher-mentor.

Needs Analysis Table B

Theme: ICT in locating and using resources
Area of development: Personal and Professional Use of ICT
Link to QTS standards: QTS standards 2002, para 2.5

Getting Started	Date/Evidence	Developing Skills	Date/Evidence	Extending Skills	Date/Evidence
I can describe the usual arrangements of computers in primary schools.		I have talked to the ICT co-ordinator about organisation of ICT resources in a school.		I have found out about equipment and software for children with Special Educational Needs.	
I can describe some of the equipment that is commonly used with computers in school.		I know how the school accesses the Internet and what arrangements are made to safeguard children.		I have visited the BECTA inclusion site and related websites.	
I have made notes on the whereabouts of the equipment in my placement school.		I have found out about any security issues with regard to accessing ICT in the school.		I have seen how ICT can be used in a targeted way within the SEN code practice.	
I have found out about the main models of use of the computers –whether in a network room, classroom or both.		I have asked about software and hardware that meets children's individual needs.		I know the location of multi-cultural and multi-faith resources on the Internet and the contribution they can make to provision.	
*If one or more of these is not yet ticked, you may find it helpful to complete the activities in 'Getting Started' on **pages 49–52**.*		*If one or more of these is not yet ticked, you may find it helpful to complete the activities in 'Developing your Skills' on **pages 81–82**.*		*If one or more of these is not yet ticked, you may find it helpful to complete the activities in 'Extending your Skills' on **pages 115–117**.*	

Chapter 2   Routine maintenance and connecting equipment

Getting to know your computer

At a basic level you need to be aware of the routine switching on, switching off and maintaining the computer you are working with. Early activities in the Getting Started chapter are simply concerned with gathering basic information and becoming acquainted with your computer.

You are more than likely to be working with an IBM compatible PC computer running some variation of the market leading Windows software. It could be that you are in a school that has a mixed economy of PC computers and some Acorn computers. Acorns were in use in many schools before the NGfL money became available and, because they are so robust and long lasting, they are still out there. They were famously powerful and easy-to-use computers with lots of high quality curriculum software, much of it written specifically for the UK education market. However, the PC has gained in predominance, not least because of the rules of competition and tendering which accompany spending on the NGfL. They have the advantage of being widely available from a range of companies. A great deal of software is available for them and they have banished many of the arcane ways of operating with recent more user-friendly, Windows operating systems.

It could be that you are working with an Apple Mac computer. The newer variants of these are iMacs and iBooks. These computers do not have a huge market share in the UK in education but are widely used in other countries in schools and colleges. They are renowned as computers for creative workplaces and graphic designers, artists, film-makers and musicians often state a preference. They are ahead of many PCs in terms of working with digital video in the curriculum (more on this in the Extending your Skills chapter) and are famously easy to use. By their own admission they have not been easy to use alongside PCs in the past. However, the situation is improving all the time and files are more easily exchanged between users of the different platforms than in the past. Some City Learning Centres, for example, have purchased hardware and software from both PC and Apple suppliers. It is true to say that there is not so much choice in terms of curriculum software. There are, however, many excellent and easy-to-use titles available.

Finally, because of their position in the marketplace, and because of the global domination of the PC market by Windows, Apple Mac computers attract fiercely loyal users who will do their best to support you if you have not used one before (if only to show you what you've been missing all these years that you have struggled with Windows!).

Computers in schools are sometimes arranged in suites known as network rooms. This means that the computers are connected together and share resources. In some cases, there are further computers in the classroom connected to the network. Where a computer does not share any resources or receive any data from another computer, where there is no physical connection to other computers nearby, it is said to be standalone. This is important to know, because it determines much about how you use the computer and maintain it on a daily basis. If it is on a network, for example, you probably save work to a user area on the server rather than to the machine in front of which you actually sit.

You may have the use of a laptop loaded with any of the operating systems already mentioned. These, like their bigger, bulkier desktop relatives can be standalone or network. Sometimes, these are networked wirelessly, without cables. People have begun to realise that there is a physical limit to the amount of space available in classrooms and plan for the greater use of portables in schools.

Getting to know the devices connected to your computer

If you are already comfortable with the basics of the computer you are working with, you will extend your skills by looking into the other pieces of equipment which may connected to it. This will include printers in the first instance but involve any number of other devices. Inevitably, the question of troubleshooting will arise and how much you are expected to be able to do in fault-finding and problem solving.

The Standards for QTS require that you are confident to perform at least basic maintenance on your computer. The limits of this technical ability are difficult to gauge. The children in your class will expect you to be able to fix more or less any problem that occurs. Later, should you become an ICT co-ordinator, your colleagues will join this band of people expectantly looking at you while you hope to rectify some issue caused by, for example, a small child inserting an eraser where a disk should go.

The point at which your technical knowledge exceeds your grasp will be defined by your own knowledge as much as anything else. The wisdom to know when to stop trying with a particular issue is as important as being able to have a go. You can create a greater number of problems by persisting with an area about which you know nothing. If you find that you are tempted to try to install some software on the school network in order to help out, please stop.

There is, or should be, a structured level of support to you as a classroom teacher. In the first instance, the ICT co-ordinator – if there is one in your school – should be able to provide some support. Their technical expertise may only just be ahead of yours. Their main role is, after all, to plan appropriately for the school's development and to provide curriculum ICT support. They should, however, have a place where you can record persistent, insoluble problems. This should then enter the province of the technician.

Schools are being encouraged to take the issue of technical support very seriously. Along with buying equipment from reputable suppliers who have been, in some way, accredited to provide to schools, comes the concept of managed services. There is an expectation that after sales service from the big companies in ICT in education should provide technical support. This works well, in many cases anyway, where the equipment is relatively new. Just as for home computers, the level of support is variable between companies and between regional offices of those companies. You will find that, just as for home use, there is a cost incurred to the school beyond the listed purchase price of the computer. Some schools have banded together to pay a salary for a technician to look after their equipment on a regular basis. One model in East London sees a technician shared between five schools. The technician makes a regular, weekly call to the employing schools and, on arrival, looks in a book to discover what tasks are necessary. There are other primary schools who have taken the unusual and expensive step of employing someone whose sole responsibility is providing support to that school, as a technician and, to an extent, as a teaching assistant during ICT lessons in a network suite.

Schools who make little or no provision for technical support are running the risk of abusing the goodwill of one or two staff who know a bit about computers and who give up what little spare time they have to fix things for people. Schools without such individuals who still make little or no provision for technical support are also running the risk of denigrating ICT as a whole in their school with consequent loss of morale and, eventually, loss of interest.

Again, as with all areas of ICT provision, there is evidence that things are improving and you can see further discussion of the issues on the BECTA website at www.becta.org.uk.

Extending technical knowledge to video and image capture

Beyond day-to-day troubleshooting lies the area of image capture from the use of scanners through to digital cameras (both still and video). There is a longer discussion of these issues in Chapter 5, Extending your Skills. It is an area of growing activity in primary schools for all sorts of reasons, not least the ease of use and much cheaper availability of the equipment.

Assessing your needs

Use the following table to determine your starting point in the activities linked to this theme in Chapters 3, 4 and 5. As soon as you have determined a starting point, go to the relevant chapter, read the background and make a start.

Remember, wherever possible, to discuss your developmental needs with a colleague, college tutor or class teacher-mentor.

Needs Analysis Table C

Theme: Routine maintenance, and connecting external equipment
Area of development: Personal and Professional Use of ICT
Link to QTS Standards: QTS Standards 2002, para 2.5

Getting Started	Date/Evidence	Developing Skills	Date/Evidence	Extending Skills	Date/Evidence
I know how to switch the computer on and off safely and the basics of health and safety with them.		I know about the difference between working on a network and working standalone.		I know how to use a digital camera and send the images to a computer.	
I have identified the make and model of the computer I'm using.		I know how to differentiate between basic hardware and software problems and how to solve them (e.g. sound failure).		I have used a scanner to capture images.	
I know where a range of commonly used peripheral devices plug into the computer.		I know how to work with different printers.		I know about the different types of image files and how to work with them.	
I can work out simple diagnostics such as why a monitor isn't displaying an image.		I know which issues are best solved by technical support and which I should be responsible for.		I have had some experience of working with video cameras and computers.	
If one or more of these is not yet ticked, you may find it helpful to complete the activities in 'Getting Started' on **pages 53–54**.		If one or more of these is not yet ticked, you may find it helpful to complete the activities in 'Developing your Skills' on **pages 83–84**.		If one or more of these is not yet ticked, you may find it helpful to complete the activities in 'Extending your Skills' on **pages 118–119**.	

Becoming part of an online community for education

Beginning to use the Internet in education

It is highly probable that you are already a user of the Internet with some inkling of the potential contribution it could make to your life as a teacher. Even if you are not, you will quickly discover that it has enormous potential as a medium of exchange for resources and ideas for teachers. You will know or discover all of this without necessarily understanding the mechanism by which it all takes place. We are all of us, to a greater or a lesser extent, in this situation with most of the technology we take for granted. How many people understand how a telephone, mobile or otherwise, works? How many people know how a television, digital or otherwise, works?

Using the Internet is in the same area of life as those other ubiquitous devices. However, knowing a little of the 'behind the scenes' activity can make our use of the Internet more efficient without necessarily confusing or misleading us.

The history of the development of the Internet from its US origins as a cold war project and evolution into an academic project and then (and now) a giant global market with library attached, is well told in books such as *The Rough Guide to the Internet* (Kennedy, 2001). This book is an excellent beginners guide to the basic concepts which have governed the Internet's growth and development and which outline its use by ordinary owners of different kinds of computers (PCs and Macs). It is not education-specific. In some ways, this is the best place to start because the Internet reaches into all aspects of life and you have a life beyond teaching (although during your training year it will not feel like it).

The Internet comprises a huge global network of computers with very fast links in between them. The links carry data in the form of words, images, video, and sound files of various kinds along cables and via satellites and distribute them worldwide. It is important to note that it is culturally dominated by its country of origin, the US. However, it is not under the direct control of any one state and any country or individual can have a presence of some sort on the Internet. It is now possible to display information in any number of different fonts and languages required by the users in those countries and from those cultures. The hardest concept to get around is the fact that the Internet does not have any real centre or regulation (beyond the registration of names of sites). This anarchic quality spawns the very best and worst of human nature and you will be aware of the concern over the vast quantities of unsuitable material flying through these cables and around the world.

For education users, the Internet represents a massive resource. Huge amounts of relevant information on any discipline are out there: reference sources, museums, maps, works of art, scientists, cultural artefacts alongside the inevitable online stores, banks and other businesses exploiting the communicative potential to reach newer and bigger markets.

The huge computers that power all of this traffic, moving and available all over the world, are attached to smaller, local networks. In turn, these provide or resell space to smaller, private, home users who connect to them and gain access to their accounts. The range of ways of gaining access to the Internet is widening and all of them have advantages and disadvantages. If you are connecting at home by dialling a number from your computer, which many people in the UK are still doing, your computer makes a temporary connection to your account on the Internet held on a bigger computer provided by your Internet Service Provider (ISP). When you have dialled the number, and your account's username and password have been verified (and all of the strange noises have stopped issuing from your computer's modem as it talks to modems at the other end) you are connected to the Internet.

If you connect to the Internet in a different way using something called ADSL or via a cable modem or satellite, your connection will always be on. You will not experience the modem dialling. Your connection will be live from when you switch the computer on because it is 'always on'. If you connect at your college or training provider's ICT provider, the chances are that they will have a fixed, permanent connection and will have provided you with an account and the software to access it. These fixed, permanent connections are many times quicker than a modem connection and make use of different types of technology. Because they are faster and have much bigger capacity these connections are capable of allowing you to see much bigger files such as video clips, sound files, animation and so on. These connections are known as broadband connections. Please don't worry about the terminology. The language used to describe the Internet and its facilities is full of strange, arcane terms and incomprehensible acronyms. Many of these are outlined in the glossary in this book and also in books such as *The Rough Guide to the Internet* (described above). You will get used to them and you will find yourself using them.

Happily, as will be seen throughout many of the activities in this book, the situation for teachers using the Internet has been made easier by the creation of lists and repositories of resources in the National Grid for Learning (NGfL). This gateway for teachers (at www.ngfl.gov.uk) provides the ideal starting point.

The ICT skills which you need for your professional use of the Internet in education, mainly comprise knowing how to navigate to websites using a Web browser and how to send messages using email. There are others, including more pro-active use, but at the beginning of your use of the Internet for education in the Getting Started chapter of this book, you will find a discussion of the basics of Web use.

Moving further with the Internet in education

In the Developing your Skills chapter in this book, there are activities within the online community theme that allow you to develop more advanced skills of using Web browsers and email. This will include developing skills of downloading freely available resources for education. In the Extending your Skills chapter, the concept of sharing expertise and making connections to other teachers is outlined. The NGfL was envisaged as an area within which teachers would discuss and exchange ideas.

This theme is part of preparing you for the future at the same time as ensuring that you develop the skills necessary to take full advantage of the massive potential of the resources and facilities online.

Assessing your needs

Use the following table to determine your starting point in the activities linked to this theme in Chapters 3, 4 and 5. As soon as you have determined a starting point, go to the relevant chapter, read the background and make a start.

Remember, wherever possible, to discuss your developmental needs with a colleague, college tutor or class teacher-mentor.

Needs analysis table D

Theme: Becoming part of an online community for education
Area of development: Personal and Professional Use of ICT
Link to QTS Standards: QTS Standards 2002, para 2.5

Getting Started	Date/Evidence	Developing Skills	Date/Evidence	Extending Skills	Date/Evidence
I know how to use a Web browser to visit different sites.		I know how to organise my Web browser with appropriate folders.		I know how to organise my email into folders. I know how to manage my address book.	
I know where the major education websites are and how to store them in the browser's favourites or bookmarks.		I know how to save resources in the form of text, images and sounds.		I know how to create a distribution list for colleagues.	
I know how to send and receive email, including how to send an attached file.		I know how to search the Internet for resources for a particular subject area.		I have visited a range of Internet projects that make use of the collaborative features of the Internet.	
I know how to make an email address that is usable from any computer on the Internet.		I know where to find materials that have been evaluated for classroom use.		I have visited a number of online communities for education. I know how to join an online forum.	
*If one or more of these is not yet ticked, you may find it helpful to complete the activities in 'Getting Started' on **pages 55–59**.*		*If one or more of these is not yet ticked, you may find it helpful to complete the activities in 'Developing your Skills' on **pages 85–88**.*		*If one or more of these is not yet ticked, you may find it helpful to complete the activities in 'Extending your Skills' on **pages 120–121**.*	

Chapter 2   Using ICT in curriculum subjects and in the Foundation Stage learning areas

Getting started in the use of ICT in the curriculum subjects at Key Stages 1 and 2, and the learning areas of the Foundation Stage, means beginning to observe the children and the adults in the school setting.

The wider context for ICT in subject teaching

You are joining the teaching profession at a time of profound and accelerated change in its relationship with ICT. Computers and computer-related equipment are ubiquitous now. Training to teach using ICT in all subjects of the curriculum is well advanced in schools across the country from a range of training providers under the New Opportunities Fund (NOF). Models of good practice exist in many LEAs and are being disseminated through the NGfL, and through BECTA (The British Educational Communications and Technology Agency) in particular. OFSTED finds year on year that the use of ICT in subject teaching is improving (although ICT itself is still the poorest taught subject, of which more later). You can research this in more depth on the OFSTED website (www.ofsted.gov.uk).

As far as the use of ICT in subject teaching is concerned, BECTA, in partnership with the University of Nottingham is managing one of the largest evaluations of learning gains with ICT ever carried out. The IMPACT2 project, due to report in the summer of 2002, has already produced interim findings, which suggest that the use of ICT has a positive effect on child attainment. You can find this and other documents, such as the *Primary Schools ICT and Standards* report along with the final IMPACT2 report on the research part of the BECTA website (www.becta.org.uk/research).

While ICT provision is being increased and its use in subject teaching continues to grow, there is no uniform level of provision across the country – for a variety of reasons to do with the complicated funding and bidding arrangements. As a consequence, you will see a variety of ages of equipment and software in a variety of settings. When you complete the activities within the theme of ICT – locating resources – you will, from your observations, have something of a context for your work in this activity. You will find, over time, that the situation is improving year on year but that some LEAs and schools still lag behind.

One context in which you will probably find yourself during placements is that of the computer suite (or network room or ICT room or any other variant of the name). In the best cases these rooms have guaranteed access and a rising standard of ICT work in subject teaching. In the worst cases there has been a tendency, in some schools, to teach discrete ICT one hour a week, empty of content from other subjects. Since ICT must have content to have any real purpose this seems to be a wasted opportunity.

The curriculum context at Key Stages 1 and 2

Your needs assessment must be informed by an appraisal of your understanding of the structure and nature of the curriculum contexts, at Key Stages 1 and 2, and in the Foundation Stage, for ICT in education.

The National Curriculum and the curriculum for the Foundation Stage lay down what is to be taught at Key Stages 1 and 2 and during Nursery and Reception. The ways in which these documents are interpreted are many and various and all have an impact on the ways in which ICT is used in the school setting.

In terms of the curriculum in Key Stages 1 and 2, you should expect to see ICT being used in all subjects. The *National Curriculum Handbook* (DfEE, 2000a for the most recent version of the National Curriculum; sometimes known as Curriculum 2000), which contains the programmes of study for all subjects, contains many examples of cross-curricular applications and states that all children should learn to use a 'range of ICT tools and information sources to support their work in other subjects' (DfEE, 2000a).

In practice there are pressures at Key Stages 1 and 2 in many schools in terms of timetabling. During the period of the introduction of the NGfL there have been two major initiatives (and several minor ones), which have had a major impact on all aspects of primary school life. The major initiatives were the National Literacy Strategy (NLS, 1998 onwards) and the National Numeracy Strategy (NNS, 1999 onwards). Massive amounts of compulsory in-service training and huge changes to the timetable (two hours of discrete literacy and numeracy every day) produced a squeeze on other subjects, including the other core subject, science, and all of the creative arts, humanities and PSHE. ICT should not have suffered to the extent that it is supposedly taught across the curriculum. However, guidance in the NLS initially contained no major reference to the use of ICT (although this has since been partially addressed with guidance on ICT in whole class teaching in the literacy hour and more to come). The NNS has been more ICT friendly with a very good set of resources issued and some exemplification in the guidance (see *Using ICT in the Daily Mathematics Lesson*, DfEE, 2000).

ICT in the *Curriculum Guidance for the Foundation Stage*

In terms of the *Curriculum Guidance for the Foundation Stage*, which emerged in 2000, there is some mention of the computer in Early Years settings. The foundation stage curriculum is organised in six areas of learning:

 ◌ personal, social and emotional development;
 ◌ language and literacy;
 ◌ mathematical development;
 ◌ knowledge and understanding of the world;
 ◌ physical development; and
 ◌ creative development.

For each of these you will be able to see opportunities for the use of ICT to support learning. Computers in Early Years settings are often incorporated into role-play areas and you could expect to see them set up as part of an office, library or doctor's surgery (or similar).

For personal, social and emotional development, you may see the computer being used as a means of getting children to work together, to take turns and share equipment. For language and literacy, you may see children exploring mark making or multimedia books and videos. For mathematical development, you may see children exploring number rhymes or games at the computer. For knowledge and understanding of the world, children can be introduced to a range of experiences from outside of the Early Years setting itself by means of the Internet or CD-ROM. For physical development, children's fine motor control could be enhanced by learning to use the mouse and the keyboard. For creative development, young children can explore the means by which images can be produced, manipulated and changed onscreen.

When you observe children working in a Foundation Stage setting, you may find that any one of those learning areas will merge and overlap with one another as they do for most learning activities in the Foundation Stage. The observational activities at each of the levels in this book give you the opportunity to see the range of interpretations there are of both guidance and order on ICT in school.

The context of teaching and learning theory

Another important context in any observation of young children learning is that of teaching and learning theory. Whichever National Curriculum order prevails at any given time there is still a need to understand what is happening at the level of the learner in the context of what we know about how children learn. Whatever the situation and whatever tool is being used by the children, it is possible to analyse the dialogue, the process and the product in relation to more than just the setting and the curriculum constraints. ICT is no exception to this, although it is sometimes made to appear that way.

What happens when children work with computers can be understood in relation to theories of how children think and learn generally. It also applies to the ways in which certain pieces of software have been designed (of which more in activities on software evaluation). For example, Piagetian theory, held that children learned in stages, building on learning, constructing their understanding of the world over time, piece by piece. Software such as Logo is directly derived from this world-view and was created by Seymour Papert who had previously worked with Jean Piaget. There will be more on this in the activities in the chapter on Developing your Skills.

If you have been introduced to social-constructivist theories of learning, you will see much in the way of work around ICT to support this view of the way children learn. Put very simply, in this theory of learning, derived from the work of Vygotsky and others, the child learns in the social context, in dialogue with more experienced learners and adults. Children make their internal speech public in conversation with others around a task, testing out their own understanding. There is an area of discourse, a zone of proximal development, in which children learn. When you observe pairs of children working at a computer, you can see this in much of the discourse between themselves and adults watching them. Charles Crook has written about the computer in this context in *Computers and the Collaborative Experience of Learning* (Crook, 1996).

Another theme derived from the work of Vygotsky is that of the child learning about the use of tools to mediate understanding and intellectual development. The case of the computer as one of the tools with which the child has to negotiate is made in the opening chapter of *Using Information Technology Effectively in Teaching and Learning* (Somekh & Davis, 1997). The teacher has a part to play and, in creating opportunities for work at the computer must exploit fully its capability to develop creative and flexible thinking as opposed to generating more 'mundane tasks which negate the opportunities for quality learning.'

By observing children working in any number of curriculum subjects and areas of learning it is possible to get to the heart of theories about teaching and learning. The computer changes the way we think and learn because it raises new ways of performing old tasks (as well as new tasks to perform). It mediates our experience of the world and forces us to look at the world differently and creatively. As teachers, we can design learning opportunities that exploit those possibilities or we can, for lack of opportunity or decent curriculum models, design activities that repeat the tasks of the past endlessly. As you have the luxury of observing children learning with computers, try to see which possibilities have been created in the different learning settings in which you find yourself.

Developing skills in the use of ICT in subject teaching

As you move on from observing the ways in which children and adults work with computers in their curriculum contexts, you will start to look at ways in which you can incorporate ICT into your own work in various subjects. Examples quoted in the relevant activities in the chapters on Developing your Skills include working with databases in mathematics and science and, when appropriate, the learning areas of the Foundation Stage.

Extending skills in the use of ICT in subject teaching

If you are comfortable with the curriculum contexts from observation and some simple exploration of the ideas, the extension is to look in more detail at the wider curriculum. Some activities in this book refer you to the curriculum strategies for the teaching of literacy and numeracy (NLS and NNS respectively). Others, like those in this theme in the Extending your Skills chapter require you to look at the other subjects in the curriculum and think about planning. Planning for ICT in the foundation subjects, as for the core curriculum means identifying those activities where ICT provides an essential part of the learning experience. In other words, it means identifying the lessons in the foundation subjects where, with ICT, the learning opportunities are enhanced in depth, range and quality. The activities themselves in this theme at this level require you to reflect on your planned use of ICT in some depth.

Assessing your needs

Use the table below to determine your starting point in the activities linked to this theme in Chapters 3, 4 and 5. As soon as you have determined a starting point, go to the relevant chapter, read the background and make a start.

Remember, wherever possible, to discuss your developmental needs with a colleague, college tutor or class teacher-mentor.

Needs Analysis Table E

Theme: Using ICT in curriculum subjects and in the learning areas of the Foundation Stage
Area of development: ICT in Subject Teaching
Link to QTS Standards: QTS Standards 2002, para 3.3.10.

Getting Started	Date/Evidence	Developing Skills	Date/Evidence	Extending Skills	Date/Evidence
I have observed children using the computer in a range of core subjects/ learning areas.		I have used a simple graphing package with children.		I am aware of the uses of ICT to support learning across the Foundation subjects or the learning areas in the Foundation Stage	
I have observed adults and how they set up computer activities for and with children.		I have interrogated a simple database with children.		I know which areas of the arts and music lend themselves to the use of ICT.	
I have watched children using ICT to support learning in creative subjects and the humanities.		I have created a database with children for use in maths and/or another area.		I know which areas of the history and geography lend themselves to the use of ICT.	
I can see how support staff can be helped to use the computer with children.		I have set up a simple spreadsheet with children to explore number patterns or simple formulae.		I can combine different sorts of files in a project for the Foundation subjects or other learning areas.	
*If one or more of these is not yet ticked, you may find it helpful to complete the activities in 'Getting Started' on **pages 60–61**.*		*If one or more of these is not yet ticked, you may find it helpful to complete the activities in 'Developing your Skills' on **pages 89–93**.*		*If one or more of these is not yet ticked, you may find it helpful to complete the activities in 'Extending your Skills' on **pages 122–127**.*	

Chapter 2   **Evaluating ICT Resources**

The skills and knowledge developed during the study of the theme of Evaluating ICT resources will help you to develop benchmarks against which to judge the usefulness and effectiveness of ICT resources of many different kinds in your subject teaching.

Software

In the Getting Started chapter you will find an activity in this theme which takes evaluating educational software as its starting point. If you have come into teaching from a background in an office environment or after using college IT facilities you will be surprised at the range of software available to support teaching in the primary school. You can find software which is targeted at every curriculum area, although as with most of primary school life at present, this is dominated by titles designed to support the core curriculum, in particular English and mathematics (now more commonly known as literacy and numeracy).

The software designed for children is of many different kinds and of equally different levels of quality. Having some kind of yardstick by which to judge educational software is essential when making both practical decisions about cost and pedagogical decisions about the way in which the software enhances teaching and learning.

Some websites are useful in providing assistance with the issues around evaluating and selecting appropriate software. One example is the TEEM (Teachers Evaluating Educational Multimedia) website where your peers in the teaching profession exchange views and suggestions about use of software. This is linked from the main NGfL website or visited direct at the following address: www.teem.org.uk. TEEM has produced guidance which can be downloaded from the site and is readily understood by teachers working in the classroom. It seeks to provide practical guidance first and foremost.

The activity linked to this theme in the Getting Started chapter looks in some detail at software categories and gives practical experience with one review framework.

Specific learning tools in curriculum use

The extension of the review concept in the Developing your Skills chapter involves an analysis of a range of specific learning tools from programmable toys through to onscreen logo. In this activity you will consider how the tools allow progression in the subjects concerned and attempt to make evaluative judgements about them as learning tools.

The subject areas under consideration are mathematics, English, geography, PSHE and ICT itself. The areas in the Foundation Stage curriculum are:

- ➲ personal, social and emotional development;
- ➲ language and literacy;
- ➲ mathematical development; and
- ➲ knowledge and understanding of the world.

The concern in this theme as a whole, whether working with the programmable toys or with onscreen logo is to look at the relationship of the ICT to the subject. Are there ways in which the subject teaching is enhanced or made possible by the use of this software in ways which were not possible before? The activity linked to this theme in the Developing your Skills chapter attempts to answer this question.

Reviewing Internet resources

The Internet has the potential to make an enormous contribution to education across the curriculum and across the age phases. Indeed, the government has spent upwards of £1.6 billion connecting schools to the National Grid for Learning (NGfL) and developing strategies to promote the development of education in an online context.

The original paper that first discussed the form and function of the NGfL, *Connecting the Learning Society*, envisaged that it would:

> 'be organised centrally into a package with links into other sites and, additionally, space for structured teacher discussion ...'(DfEE, 1997).

Beyond the mere provision of links into other sites was the idea that there would be online discussion and interaction. Part of the entitlement for a teacher in the era of the NGfL would be the opportunity to go online and share ideas and explore issues with fellow professionals.

Furthermore, and central to current developments, there was an emphasis on the provision of resources for use in schools and in the wider community. Teachers in various settings around the country and beyond the UK education system increasingly make resources available to their colleagues. These can take the form of lesson plans, worksheets, animations, movie clips, technical tips and notes. There is official provision for this in the Teacher Resource Exchange (follow the link from the BECTA website – www.becta.org.uk). Other sites have emerged which are either semi-official or the work of enthusiasts. Sometimes these are produced under the auspices of local authority grids within the NGfL (The Kent Grid for Learning would be an example – follow the link from the NGfL A–Z page).

A large and growing collection of sites carry official recommendations from the NGfL but charge a subscription to schools. Sometimes these have selections from their resources free but charge for the majority of their material. Sometimes they are provided by the supplier of the network and/or Internet connection being used by the school. Research Machines (RM) is an example of a supplier of such subscription material.

Finally, aiming to make full use of faster Internet access, is an initiative known as 'Curriculum Online'. This is described in the DfES document *Transforming the way we learn* (DfES, 2002), which sets out a vision for the production of high quality digital resources available for distribution in the NGfL. It is anticipated that these will be available late in 2002.

Considering issues of safety

The Internet is an environment in which children can be vulnerable. Embracing the many potential resources being created and distributed online also means being aware of the potential risks. Schools must have an 'acceptable use' policy which describes how children are protected from unsuitable material and from the issue of casual, potentially dangerous, contact with strangers in email and chat rooms. The activity in the chapter, Extending your Skills, asks you to investigate how access to the Internet is organised in schools to address such safety issues.

Assessing your needs

Use the following table to determine your starting point in the activities linked to this theme In Chapters 3, 4 and 5. As soon as you have determined a starting point, go to the relevant chapter, read the background and make a start.

Remember, wherever possible, to discuss your developmental needs with a colleague, college tutor or class teacher-mentor.

Needs analysis table F

Theme: Evaluating ICT Resources
Area of development: ICT in Subject Teaching
Link to QTS Standards: QTS Standards 2002, para 3.3.10

Getting Started	Date/Evidence	Developing Skills	Date/Evidence	Extending Skills	Date/Evidence
I can sort software into different sorts of categories by subject.		Based on observation, I can make some judgements about the learning going on around a particular ICT resource.		I know where to locate suitable educational resources in the NGfL.	
I can sort software into different sorts of categories by method of use.		I have used specific learning tools with children, including a floor robot in maths/geography or Foundation Stage learning area.		I know how to evaluate a range of resources on the Internet against suitable criteria.	
I can make judgements about the suitability of a piece of software for a particular age.		I have observed children using software designed to work with curriculum initiatives such as the literacy hour.		I am aware of the safety issues with regard to the use of the Internet.	
Based on observation, I can make judgements about the success or otherwise of a piece of software with a group of children.		I have observed children working with tutorial software, possibly including ILS.		I have used websites which reflect different teaching and learning styles.	
*If one or more of these is not yet ticked, you may find it helpful to complete the activities in 'Getting Started' on **pages 62–64**.*		*If one or more of these is not yet ticked, you may find it helpful to complete the activities in 'Developing your Skills' on **pages 94–95**.*		*If one or more of these is not yet ticked, you may find it helpful to complete the activities in 'Extending your Skills' on **pages 128–129**.*	

Chapter 2   Making the connections between subject schemes and plans

This theme is concerned with seeing the possibilities for the use of ICT resources in subject areas. It builds on activities linked to the previous theme (Evaluating ICT resources) and seeks to provide connections with particular subject schemes of work and initiatives. For the Foundation Stage, it considers which areas of learning will be most appropriate to which ICT resources.

In the activities in the Getting Started chapter linked to this theme, you will try to match software to curriculum areas at a fairly basic level. For this purpose, it will be necessary to adopt some categories of software by type, as follows:

⊃ *Content-rich resources*. These are software titles with specific subject-related or reference content. Examples of content-rich resources would include encyclopaedias, dictionaries, atlases and so on.
⊃ *Tools*. These are sometimes known as 'content-free resources', although 'tools' is the preferred terminology. These are software titles which allow for tasks to be performed by the child. Examples would be word processors, spreadsheets, presentation software, multimedia software, iMovie and so on.
⊃ *Courseware*. These are also known as tutorial software titles. These contain specific tutorial content to support a curriculum area. For younger children this might include aspects of phonics and reading. For older children this might include more complex grammatical work or work to support a particular science concept.
⊃ *Assessment software*. These sorts of titles aim to support SATS and other forms of assessment.

Throughout this theme there will be practical considerations of organisational issues within the school. There is a strong relationship between work in this theme and work in the theme on ICT in locating and using resources (see **pages 12–14** above).

The National Literacy Strategy (NLS) and ICT

The National Literacy Strategy (NLS) Framework as it was originally issued is now established in most primary schools in the UK. Where a school does not use the NLS, it will be using a local or school-based strategy of equivalent breadth and resource. Over time, the NLS is undergoing revision and changes in emphasis, in particular in response to the concern about attainment levels in writing. Furthermore, in Curriculum 2000 it is explicitly stated that the framework:

> *'provides a detailed basis for implementing the statutory requirements of the programmes of study for reading and writing' (QCA, 2000a).*

In other words, the NLS is a de facto scheme of work for some, perhaps not all, of the National Curriculum subject of English. Given that ICT should be used in every subject scheme of work, it must also have a place in the literacy hour itself. There is clearly a need to begin to address what ICT can do alongside the framework in helping to raise levels of achievement in literacy.

The framework, with which trainees will become very familiar during their training in English, outlines the activities in literacy by year group from Year 1 to Year 6, over each of the terms of the school year. There are materials for Reception which are also in use in some schools, although there will be a change in emphasis as the Curriculum Guidance for the Foundation Stage is adopted in schools.

The issue for those attempting to work with ICT in the literacy hour is how to integrate it into the very tight timescales which have been prescribed. The solution to this issue will, as usual, be different in almost every setting, and contingent upon the resources available in all the categories: human resources, hardware resources and software resources.

There is some guidance available now for the use of ICT in the whole class elements of the literacy hour called *ICT in the Literacy Hour: Whole Class Teaching*, published by the DfES (DfES, 2001a).

The outline of the literacy hour is as follows:

The first ten to fifteen minutes outlines the work of the day in terms of word level or sentence level. The next fifteen minutes focuses on an aspect of word level work (Key Stage 1) and sentence or word level work (Key Stage 2). Up to this point in the basic model of provision, children have been sitting on the carpet for half an hour. For the next twenty minutes, children move to their tables to undertake group activities in fives and sixes related to the overall learning objective. Finally, there is a plenary, lasting approximately ten minutes. This attempts to draw the strands from the hour together and to underline key teaching points with the children.

The twenty minutes of group activity lends itself best to the use of the computer. In a low-resource setting – with one computer in the corner of the classroom – there will need to be some creativity with the planning. Depending on the nature of the task and the nature of the software being used, it could be possible to split a group of six into two lots of three with ten minutes each. This group would then become part of the working week in the normal way and the whole class rotated through in a week.

In some ways, this is an example of the atomised curriculum at its worst, with children not being able to develop any real ICT skills in such short bursts. It also has high planning overheads because of the need to think of something purposeful for the children to do while they are waiting for their turn. On the other hand, there are some useful activities which lend themselves to shorter amounts of time at the computer. In Courseware on CD there might be short activities and investigations around a particular learning objective. An onscreen exercise, for example, to identify parts of words and break them down into constituent sounds would be one. Clearly, pointing and clicking on items in a menu or a game in such software is not doing a great deal to advance the knowledge and understanding of ICT. However, the literacy hour provision itself might be enhanced by the regular presence of reinforcement of learning objectives which are different from the daily diet of photocopied worksheets.

Another idea is to use open-ended software in this situation to create your own short activities. Using a word processor, a document template could be created which allowed children to, for example, search and replace nouns with pronouns. Another could allow children to highlight all the verbs in a sentence in sentence level work and change the font in some way. At this level of resourcing, activities are going to be low level with some element of repetition and reinforcement. However, in this example, with open-ended software, the ICT is being used to provide stimulus and variety and one more planning option for the hard pressed class teacher. It can also legitimately be said to be providing variety for the children and a further opportunity to address child learning styles.

If you have access to presentation software and the computer is accessible to the carpet area then, in a given week, children could be preparing small presentations on the learning objective for the plenary each day (examples of this can be found on the NLS CD-ROM (DfES, 2001a)). This is potentially the highest order development of ICT skills, perhaps also of the literacy focus. As the class teacher, familiar with the children concerned, you would be in a position to determine which of the children would benefit from this. It need not always be the most able. In this situation, having an adult helper who is also familiar with the software (cf. human resources in previous sections) would allow the children who are struggling with a given concept to reinforce their learning by having to construct a presentation for others.

Where a school has very rich provision for ICT, there is inevitably more room for using ICT in the literacy hour.

In the simplest example, if there are more computers in the classroom (perhaps three) then a group can go on in pairs for the whole of the twenty minutes of group activity, undertaking any of the examples illustrated above at a higher level due to the extended time available.

If the high resource setting manifests itself in the form of a collection of handheld computers, there is very great potential. A group of six children can have access to search and replace activities on the palmtops as well as onscreen templates of various kinds. Children can also undertake guided writing with adult support if this is appropriate. This activity can become part of the cycle of activities during the week, perhaps combined with the uses of the desktop described above.

In an ICT suite, it would be possible to run the entire literacy hour in there at regular intervals. Each child would have access to the computers, plenaries could be held using the large monitors or whiteboards (if available) or screen control software. The opening sections of the literacy hour could be presented to the children using hypermedia resources, perhaps containing scanned parts of books for the big book part of the session. These activities have a high overhead in terms of staff training and confidence. In a high resource setting where training has taken place which fully integrates ICT into the good practice of the school and where the children are using the network room confidently, ICT has much to offer the literacy hour, specifically it:

➲ provides a different resource base for the literacy hour, a break from the classroom;
➲ allows children to develop ICT skills alongside literacy skills (except in the case of tutorial software);
➲ reinforces the message that ICT is a medium in which to carry out different kinds of work; and
➲ provides the opportunity for children to combine text, graphics, sound and video in different software packages.

The Internet, in a high-resource setting, is an area of real potential. Very large numbers of teachers and children are already online, sharing ideas for lesson plans. Many of these are downloadable without charge and provide a basis for planning (for more information on this, see the activities linked to the theme on Using the Internet on **pages 85–88**).

Other sites provide onscreen activities with immediate feedback, all of them directly related to the literacy hour framework.

School webpages or LEA intranets can provide rich sources of material and opportunities for publication, including many examples of good practice in the literacy hour.

There are similar issues for the use of ICT in the daily mathematics lesson (the mathematics equivalent to the literacy hour). There are however, some important differences which are discussed further in the background to the activity linked to this theme in the Developing your Skills chapter on **pages 96–97**.

In the Extending your Skills chapter, there is an activity which asks you to use ICT to combine subject areas in ways suggested by some of the latest evaluations of, for example, the National Literacy Strategy.

Assessing your needs

Use the following table to determine your starting point in the activities linked to this theme in Chapters 3, 4 and 5. As soon as you have determined a starting point, go to the relevant chapter, read the background and make a start.

Remember, wherever possible, to discuss your developmental needs with a colleague, college tutor or class teacher-mentor.

Needs analysis table G

Theme: Making the connections between subject schemes and plans
Area of development: ICT in Subject Teaching
Link to QTS Standards: QTS Standards 2002, para 3.3.10

Getting Started	Date/Evidence	Developing Skills	Date/Evidence	Extending Skills	Date/Evidence
I have made a list of the available software in a school by subject area.		I have read appropriate guidance on how to use ICT in the curriculum strategies.		I have planned and evaluated work with ICT in science and/ or Foundation subjects.	
I am aware of the schemes of work for core curriculum areas and how they can be supported by software.		I have planned and evaluated work with ICT in the literacy hour opening or closing sections.		I have started planning for subject teaching and regularly including opportunities for ICT.	
I have seen how the scheme of work can be supported by appropriate software and websites.		I have devised group work in literacy with ICT.		I have looked at exemplar material on the Internet for using ICT in subject teaching and I have evaluated it.	
I have reviewed websites for curriculum content appropriate to schemes of work.		I have devised and evaluated ICT work which supports learning in the daily maths lesson.		I have produced a short scheme of work in one curriculum or learning area that makes central use of ICT.	
*If one or more of these is not yet ticked, you may find it helpful to complete the activities in 'Getting Started' on **pages 65–66**.*		*If one or more of these is not yet ticked, you may find it helpful to complete the activities in 'Developing your Skills' on **pages 96–98**.*		*If one or more of these is not yet ticked, you may find it helpful to complete the activities in 'Extending your Skills' on **pages 130–132**.*	

Chapter 2 Progression, continuity and issues of assessment in ICT

This theme is all about beginning to consider the issues of ICT as a subject in its own right with its own set of skills and knowledge. ICT requires a context and a purpose and, in a school, this is most often provided by its use in other subjects. In fact, the orders for every subject require ICT to be used (see the *National Curriculum Handbook*, DfEE, 2000).

However, ICT is a subject in its own right with its own history and its own pedagogical debates. It also has its own set of National Curriculum orders and, as a teacher, you will need to be mindful of which sorts of skills, and which sets of knowledge, of ICT are being developed by children during their primary school years. As a teacher of Foundation Stage children, you will need to be equally aware of the children's earliest ICT experiences and how they may be incorporated into the world of the Early Years.

ICT as a subject at Key Stages 1 and 2

The *National Curriculum Handbook* (DfEE, 2000a) specifies what must be taught in schools and contains programmes of study which must be followed in each subject. It does not set out how this should be achieved. Schools and LEAs are free to make their own choices about the path that is followed in covering the content of the National Curriculum Orders in the various subjects.

The government has, however, issued schemes of work for subjects which divide the content up into units and which suggest activities leading to the coverage of all elements of the programmes of study. For English and mathematics, the National Literacy Strategy and National Numeracy Strategy represent possible schemes of work in those subjects. For all other subjects there is considerable guidance in the form of subject schemes available in paper form or from the Internet.

ICT is no exception. Since 1998 there has been guidance providing a map of learning and a suggested path of continuity and progression which schools can follow in covering the National Curriculum. At that time, before the subject was revised and renamed in the revised National Curriculum, the scheme of work was for information technology. The scheme of work was reissued with some changes by the DfEE and Qualifications and Curriculum Authority (QCA) in 2000 when the subject simultaneously became information and communication technology (ICT).

Schools and LEAs are not required to follow the QCA scheme of work to the letter. Many schools adapt the content to suit their local needs or write a completely new scheme. One example would be the London Borough of Newham which has its own scheme of work (see samples at http://itass.newham.gov.uk/curric). If a school or LEA decides to go its own way, however, it must still operate a scheme which is at least as comprehensive in its coverage of the National Curriculum as the QCA document. The scheme must demonstrate to OFSTED, for example, that it provides continuity, progression and assessment opportunities which lead to good teaching and learning of, and with, ICT.

In the *National Curriculum Handbook* (DfEE, 2000a), ICT is organised under four headings, with a further set of statements specifying the 'breadth of study'. The four headings in Curriculum 2000 describe what should be studied by all children in schools in England. Working with them means finding curricular opportunities within ICT as a subject and within ICT in subject teaching to develop their skills under the headings of:

➲ finding things out;

⊃ developing ideas and making things happen;
⊃ exchanging and sharing information;
⊃ reviewing, modifying and evaluating work as it progresses.

The scheme of work sets out a series of units from Years 1 to 5 arranged to work on elements of these headings progressively and simultaneously. Coverage is mapped out on an index card at the front of the scheme of work folder.

To give a concrete example: if you were a teacher of a Year 3 class and you were working on the first of the five units in the scheme for Year 3 ('Combining Text and Graphics'), you could locate which parts of the National Curriculum were being covered on the card at the front of the QCA scheme of work. Reading from the table you would find that this unit is intended to cover Key Stage 2 programmes of study 2a, 3a and 4b.

If you have the handbook nearby, or if you have an electronic copy, you can find that the unit, 'Combining Text and Graphics' at Year 3 is expected to address development in the following elements of the programmes of study (from 'Developing ideas and making things happen'):

2 Pupils should be taught:
a) to use text, tables, images and sound to develop their ideas.

From 'Exchanging and sharing information':

3. Pupils should be taught:
a) how to share their ideas by presenting information in a variety of forms [for example, text, images, tables, sounds].

From 'Reviewing, modifying and evaluating work as it progresses':

4. Pupils should be taught to:
b) describe the effects of their actions.

Clearly, the 'QCA scheme of work for ICT' (DfEE, 2000c) is a useful planning tool in terms of coverage of the National Curriculum. Does it help with any of the detail of your planning? How does the document work in practice?

Like any other document used for planning there is a learning curve. However, the more you use the document, the more familiar the language and the layout becomes. On the first page is the unit title. The letters are not there to indicate any particular order in which the units should be taught. Underneath the title is a section labelled 'About the Unit' which gives an overview of the unit. This is followed by descriptions of the unit in relation to other parts of the scheme ('Where The Unit Fits In'), the vocabulary you need to introduce to the children ('Technical Vocabulary' – similar in concept to the National Literacy Strategy vocabulary lists), and, the resources you will need ('Resources', both computer based and other forms of technology).

The element of differentiation is supplied in the section labelled 'Expectations'. This is a series of outcomes for 'most children', 'some children [who] will not have made so much progress' and 'some [who] will have progressed further'. These broad statements require much greater fine tuning at the classroom level.

The unit descriptions continue across the A3 sheet on the following sides under four headings:

1 learning objectives;
2 possible teaching activities;
3 learning outcomes; and
4 points to note.

'Learning objectives' outlines the steps towards full understanding of the unit. 'Possible teaching activities' are described under three potential headings (see below). 'Learning outcomes' describes the indications of a child's progress and are intended to inform assessment (see chapter on assessment for a much more detailed discussion of this element). 'Points to note' outlines the misconceptions which a child may have and includes suggestions to overcome these issues.

As stated above, 'possible teaching activities' are further grouped under three different types of teaching activities:

1 setting the scene – introducing the unit to the children and taking only a few minutes;
2 short focused tasks – instructing on a specific ICT task and introducing key ideas such as cutting, copying and pasting; and
3 integrated tasks – more complex projects which build on the shorter tasks and require several sessions to complete.

The units of work are adaptable to the range of resource settings in which you will find yourself. The activity linked to this theme in the Getting Started chapter in this book is a familiarisation activity.

The Foundation Stage and ICT

If you are working in the Foundation Stage, the document used for determining the curriculum for Reception and Nursery aged children is the Curriculum for the Foundation Stage. This is not addressed by the QCA scheme of work which is concerned with KS1 and 2 (children aged from 5–11).

In Early Years settings covered by the Foundation Stage curriculum there is much scope for using ICT in each of the six learning areas. From the planning point of view it is important to be clear about how each of the defined areas of learning can be enriched and enhanced by ICT. It means thinking about the computer in each of the six contexts:

1 personal, social and emotional development;
2 communication, language and literacy;
3 mathematical development;
4 knowledge and understanding of the world;
5 physical development;
6 creative development.

Personal, social and emotional development

To address this learning area, you may want to plan opportunities for any of the following to occur:

➲ learning how to share the equipment and take turns (particularly with such a motivating and attractive resource), in other words using the computer to allow children to establish constructive relationships with each other and with other adults;
➲ using the computer to encourage collaboration between children and between adults and children in problem solving (even at the basic level of switching on, selecting an item from a menu, clicking on a name);
➲ using the computer to explore worlds beyond the Early Years setting through the Internet or CD-ROM; and
➲ using the computer as a tool to encourage collaboration between children who are experiencing difficulties and others in the Early Years setting (using alternative access devices alongside mice and keyboards).

Communication, language and literacy

Encouraging children's development of this learning area in the Early Years setting with the computer means planning opportunities for children to:

➲ write messages, label pictures with their name and otherwise engage with the communicative aspects of ICT. They do not have to get it right in the same way as a writing area doesn't exclude children who can't yet form letters. The uncritical nature of the ICT can prove extremely motivating (particularly when the computer is in a role play area and the child is experiencing an impetus to try from the imaginative play);
➲ experience the notion that computers can communicate words and pictures from books. If an adult helper, parent, older child is present, much useful talk and discussion about books and print, words and sounds, computers and communication can occur; and
➲ communicate with friends, relatives, peers in other settings nearby and very far away if possible. Children know that the computer is one among many tools for communication over distance and time. If the computer cannot deliver the

necessary experiences then other ICT equipment such as a digital camera, video camera, tape recorder may be able to.

Mathematical development

For this learning area, the following opportunities might be useful:

⊃ plan to use software which allows children to experience situations of counting and sharing and identifying numbers e.g. in counting items for a picnic. The most enduring and widely used Early Years software appears to be amongst the most simple and involves such activities as identifying numbers and counting items; and

⊃ use software which relates a counting song or nursery rhyme known to the children to reinforce early counting concepts and which allows the children to have some free play. If children are working with parent helpers or other adults and making conscious what they understand, much constructive dialogue can take place which takes the child forward.

Knowledge and understanding of the world

ICT can develop the skills of enquiry and of building understanding of the world in the Early Years setting in many ways. There are specific references to the use of ICT in this learning area in the *Curriculum Guidance for the Foundation Stage* (DfEE, 2000b pages 92–93). Activities are introduced which allow children to work with programmable toys (cf. Activity 2G). There is also the suggestion that children get to know that ICT is about more than just computers. They see the whole range of devices (cf. Activity 1J).

The following might be used to plan to address this key learning area:

⊃ set up the computer within a role play area. Consider settings with which the children are familiar such as libraries, doctors' surgeries, any kind of office. This creates a powerful context for imaginative play because the computer reinforces the 'reality' of the situation for the child. It is a powerful stimulus for the inner speech and the outer dialogue in the zone of proximal development.

The computer provides everyone in the Early Years setting with a means of recording in writing, orally and visually (still and full motion), the children's experiences as learners. Digital cameras are highly significant tools in this context, with their capacity for immediate feedback.

The capacity for ICT to provide access to activities for many children with special educational needs (including sensory impairment, physical and behavioural problems) allows for activities which promote knowledge and understanding of the world to be planned for all.

As mentioned in the context of personal, social and emotional development, there is plenty of scope for the Internet and CD-ROMs to bring experiences of other cultures and other worlds into the Early Years setting.

Physical development

This learning area can be planned for in terms of computer use with the following considerations in mind:

⊃ use of ICT equipment to promote and develop fine motor skills, in particular, the use of the mouse; and

⊃ for children who are experiencing difficulties in fine motor skills across the whole range of severity, access devices such as, brightly coloured, larger keyboards, touch windows and trackballs can all be used. Concept Keyboards which contain teacher-defined touch areas, touch screens and big switches which can be wheelchair mounted and others all allow for inclusion and development within the Early Years setting.

Creative development

ICT can bring experiences with new media which can be used alongside the range of traditional, hands-on experiences. For example:

⊃ the use of graphics software is an area of great potential in the Early Years setting. The medium in which the learner operates is infinitely editable and scalable. Colours in huge areas of the onscreen canvas can be varied at the click of a mouse. Shapes can be created with and without filled areas. With support from an adult or working with a friend the child can be encouraged to verbalise their thoughts on the image they are making. Digital cameras allow images of the child themselves to become part of the onscreen canvas; and

➲ ICT also offers the Early Years setting the potential to be creative with sound and with video. Simple musical composition software allows young learners to see that you can do more than just paint and write at a computer. A recording studio is another imaginary scenario in which to explore and develop.

Assessing children's ICT skills

As you become familiar with ICT as a subject in its own right at Key Stages 1 and 2 (or as a part of the learning provision in the Foundation Stage in its own right), you will appreciate the need for a framework for assessment of developing skills. The activity in the Developing your Skills chapter linked to this theme allows you to develop an understanding of the issues. There is a detailed discussion of issues of assessment in ICT in the background to the activity on **pages 94–95**. The activity linked to this theme in Extending your Skills takes the ideas a stage further with a look at progression and continuity in ICT across the whole school (see **pages 99–101**).

Assessing your needs

Use the following table to determine your starting point in the activities linked to this theme in Chapters 3, 4 and 5. As soon as you have determined a starting point, go to the relevant chapter, read the background and make a start.

Remember, wherever possible, to discuss your developmental needs with a colleague, college tutor or class teacher-mentor.

Needs analysis table G

Theme: Progression, continuity and issues of assessment in ICT
Area of development: ICT as a subject in its own right
Link to QTS Standards: QTS Standards 2002, para. 2.1 b

Getting Started	Date/Evidence	Developing Skills	Date/Evidence	Extending Skills	Date/Evidence
I am aware of the content and structure of the National Curriculum for ICT as a subject.		I have observed a small group of children working with ICT in order to assess their approximate level of skill.		I have read texts on ICT in teaching and learning.	
I am aware of the organisation of the QCA scheme of work for ICT.		I have analysed children's conceptions of computers and have used this knowledge in my planning.		I have interviewed the ICT co-ordinator about the scheme of work at the school.	
I have talked to the ICT co-ordinator about how ICT is organised in the school and which scheme of work is being followed.		I have used simple tracking systems of children's ICT skills.		I have looked at research on the Internet in the effectiveness of teaching and learning with ICT.	
I am aware of the potential uses of ICT in the Foundation Stage learning areas.		I have observed ICT work out of my usual age phase so that I can understand issues of progression.		I am aware of the recent inspection evidence on ICT in schools from OFSTED and elsewhere.	
*If one or more of these is not yet ticked, you may find it helpful to complete the activities in 'Getting Started' on **pages 67–68**.*		*If one or more of these is not yet ticked, you may find it helpful to complete the activities in 'Developing your Skills' on **pages 99–102**.*		*If one or more of these is not yet ticked, you may find it helpful to complete the activities in 'Extending your Skills' on **pages 133–134**.*	

Chapter 2 — Developing children's ICT skills

This theme is concerned with having organisational and planning strategies in place which allow you to develop children's ICT concepts and skills. In fact, the overall aim for working with ICT as a subject in its own right, even when supporting and enhancing other curriculum areas, is to deepen those concepts and skills. As discussed in the sections on your own personal use of ICT (see ICT in planning and assessment **pages 9–11**) much of this is to do with knowing how to create, save, access and change files of all kinds which you have made.

On a regular basis and always with new computer programmes in the classroom, arrange a whole class session. In a low resource setting i.e. a single computer to a class of thirty children, first bring the computer to the carpet area where it can be seen by everybody. This immediately brings the computer out of its corner and into the world of the classroom.

The aim is to allow the computer to come into the world of the classroom more fully. A question and answer style lends itself to this situation. Allow the children to contribute, even to provide tips for other users. Discuss with them the difficulties that they have overcome in familiarising themselves with the onscreen layout of the particular piece of software. Whole class sessions can be enhanced by the following examples and principles.

➲ Ask the children to discover during the session, and then report back on, different ways of doing the same thing. In a writing program for example, how to make text appear in a different font size or colour.
➲ Stress regular, practical instructions by giving a mantra-like tone to them. One such regularly repeated instruction should be 'Save Before You Print', droned to children day in, day out in order to persuade them that they should indeed save before they print in order to avoid the inevitable heartache which arises when a document gets lost in a malfunctioning printer.
➲ As is the case with all good primary practice, question children who don't always jump up and down with the answer (don't favour the loud over the quiet).
➲ Invite children to contribute to the discussion, strictly girl –boy – girl – boy etc.
➲ Do not allow one sex or group of children to dominate.
➲ Stress the team building aspects of sharing strategies so that they/we can all use the computer efficiently and safely.
➲ Involve children in a discussion about safety – monitor position, length of time, seating and so on.
➲ Let everyone become an expert.
➲ Value what they say even when it is patently wrong. Help them to discover a better way constructively (That's a good suggestion but…).

Regular whole class input increases the shared level of knowledge in the classroom about the use of the computer. It increases the overall standard of ICT work and the number of areas for which you can use ICT with some feeling of security.

Becoming independent and increasingly competent in basic ICT skills will engender in the children a sense of responsibility for their work. From an early age, as children progress through the school, they are expected to take on more responsibility for knowing where their equipment is, where their possessions are, where they're going next and so on. It should be the same for ICT. Children can be shown the importance of looking after electronic forms of their work, just as they can the importance of looking after their draft books. They will need to be shown how to save and retrieve their work and the importance of backing up work.

All of these activities allow you and the children to start to think of the computer as more a part of the world of the classroom. More than that, they foster a belief amongst all users in the classroom that they can become competent and confident manipulators of ICT.

The alternative model of instruction, a version of the cascade model, whereby one or two children learn it and teach others over a period of time discreetly while other children get on with the real work allows the more negative messages about ICT to be disseminated. Amongst these more negative messages are:

1   There are ICT experts who know everything and must always be consulted before you do anything.
2   ICT is something that happens in a corner of the room away from the mainstream and is never discussed and nothing to do with the rest of the school day.

Show children that you are also a learner. ICT will be less threatening to you as a teacher if you enter into the situation as a learner alongside them. It is wrong to give children the impression that you or anyone else knows all they need to know about computers. Frustrating as it may be, the truth of the matter is that we are all always learning about ICT. Once one thing is learned you can be sure another parameter will enter the equation. It is OK to make mistakes. If the basic care of the equipment is known and respected, there is not much harm that can be done.

At the same time it is important in the low resource setting to establish and maintain a rota. Rotas ensure that there is equality of access and of opportunity in the classroom. However, they should not be fixed once and for all at the start of an academic year. The acquisition of ICT skills is a dynamic process, always changing. After whole class input, in the beginning of working with a new piece of software or hardware, children need time to practise. Longer rota periods can be gradually shortened as children gain more skills.

Rotas should always be public. They should be large, on the wall, clearly visible so that children can see that there is equality of provision. Older children can be involved in the drawing up and monitoring of time on the system. With software which has specific content, such as a game or simulation or where the software is of the Drill and Practice sort –such as Integrated Learning Systems, there are fixed, tighter, more specific timetables of use involved. These are monitored by the software itself.

Many of the same principles from the previous section apply in networked computer suites.

In a High Resource Setting, it is quite likely that you will be able to show all the children exactly what the session is about by means of a large display. This will be in the form of a large monitor, projector onto a screen or an interactive electronic whiteboard. It could be by being able to take control of the screens at the individual stations and replacing them with the teaching screen via some network software. In schools where there is no such display facility you will have to gather the children together in a space in front of one of the monitors. Teaching in network rooms without a large display is very difficult.

There are additional levels of complexity in network rooms and you must be on the alert for children who are still thinking in terms of standalone use. In the first place, make use of the large display or screen grabbing facility to demonstrate the procedure for logging on. Remind the children that they do not have to sit at the same machine each week. Remind them about the importance of their password. Here are some different models of practice:

⮑ whole class logon with the same username and password into a general area on the network for that class;
⮑ children have a unique username and password;
⮑ children have group logon names and passwords.

Before teaching the children on a network, make sure that you understand the process of logging on yourself. Ask the ICT co-ordinator (or technician) before starting (remember to ask for your own username and password as a guest on placement at the school!). Children are often given their own area on the network in which to save their work. It is important that you follow the same protocols as they are used to.

As a rule, unless the children are very young, they should be taught how to log on and log off their network. This is part of learning about network literacy, a concept that is new to primary schools where previously children and teachers worked with one standalone computer in the corner of the classroom. One strategy is to have all the passwords and usernames on index cards, used at the beginning of the session and collected at the end.

Whole class demonstrations can, and should, still take place. But they need to be a sensible length, enabling the children to make the best use of what may be their only time in the week when they are on the machines. After all, lesson management ought to be easier with no other activities going on other than computing. The teacher can provide more direct input for the children. Where these grouped computers are networked, saving and logging of progress is even easier.

Further skills development

In activities linked to this theme in the Developing your Skills chapter, you will consider how to encourage children to connect their developing skills in ICT and to become aware of ICT as a subject in its own right, with its own skill sets, knowledge and vocabulary. In Extending your Skills, you will consider how their development sits within the wider, national context of ICT as a subject in its own right.

Assessing your needs

Use the table below to determine your starting point in the activities linked to this theme in Chapters 3, 4 and 5. As soon as you have determined a starting point, go to the relevant chapter, read the background and make a start.

Remember, wherever possible, to discuss your developmental needs with a colleague, college tutor or class teacher-mentor.

Needs analysis table I

Theme: Developing children's ICT skills
Area of development: ICT as a subject in its own right
Link to QTS Standards: QTS Standards 2002, para. 2.1 b

Getting Started	Date/Evidence	Developing Skills	Date/Evidence	Extending Skills	Date/Evidence
I have asked the children about the uses of the computer in the outside world.		I have used a range of ICT tools with children.		I have produced evaluations of my teaching with ICT.	
I have established regular routines and sharing of tips about computer use.		I have discussed the different sorts of peripheral equipment which can be used with computers.		I have begun to revise planning in the light of evaluation.	
On outings I have pointed out the use of computers in other settings.		I have talked with children about the suitability of hardware and software for the given task.		I have used questioning to discover children's developing concepts and misconceptions.	
I have provided books and other resources about the use of computers in the outside world.		I have involved children in the choices of particular ICT tools for particular tasks.		I have used concept maps to analyse children's developing concepts and misconceptions.	
*If one or more of these is not yet ticked, you may find it helpful to complete the activities in 'Getting Started' on **pages 69–70**.*		*If one or more of these is not yet ticked, you may find it helpful to complete the activities in 'Developing your Skills' on **pages 103–105**.*		*If one or more of these is not yet ticked, you may find it helpful to complete the activities in 'Extending your Skills' on **pages 135–136**.*	

Developing children's ability to make connections and solve problems

In their primary school years, children will see ICT as a tool, as a source of reference material and as a vehicle for delivering tutorial content. Part of developing children's subject knowledge with ICT means drawing their attention to the uses of ICT in the world outside school. The curriculum for ICT as a subject in its own right incorporates the use of ICT in the world outside school as a major component of the work you carry out with them.

For children in Key Stage 1 this means that:

'pupils should be taught knowledge, skills and understanding [in ICT] through … talking about the uses of ICT inside and outside school.'

And for children in Key Stage 2 this means extending discussions to:

'investigating and comparing the uses of ICT inside and outside school' (DfEE, 2000a).

For children in the Foundation Stage, drawing their attention to real and work-related purposes for the use of ICT is not formalised into discrete elements. It is incorporated into the various learning areas and includes opportunities, for example, for building ICT into role-play areas.

In all stages children need to be aware of the fact that ICT is widely used in a range of contexts such as doctors' surgeries, libraries, schools, in the media, in the home and so on. They also need to be reminded that the range of ICT includes not only computers but also devices such as DVD players, video cameras, video recorders and so on. The activity in the Getting Started chapter linked to this theme, begins with a brainstorm which suggests that you record what children know about the various forms of ICT.

Each time ICT is used there is an opportunity to develop children's understanding of how it is used to solve problems in the outside world by broadening the discussion into the use of the computer in that particular context. This encourages children to think more creatively and flexibly about the ICT they are using. Discussion should always be critical in nature and should include examples of ICT not working so well and what can be done about it.

One example would be working with databases with older children. You could draw their attention to areas of life in which databases figure strongly. This could be as simple as discussing the register with them. After all, it is a data-handling activity in which they engage every single day of their school life. They know that records of their attendance and punctuality are held on them. The second part of the activity linked to this theme in the Getting Started chapter suggests that you broaden the discussion into much wider areas.

Another way of relating real and work-related examples of ICT to the work that children undertake is to bring digital media into the realm of the classroom. By putting the tools of such media into their hands you are empowering children to become active in an area of life in which they are mostly encouraged to be passive consumers.

This approach is developed further in the Developing your Skills chapter with an activity requiring children to combine skills and knowledge gained in ICT in work with presentation and desktop publishing software.

In Extending your Skills, there is an activity requiring you to work with children to combine skills and knowledge gained in ICT in work with hypermedia and webpage authoring. Further background is provided on **pages 137–139**.

Assessing your needs

Use the table below to determine your starting point in the activities linked to this theme in Chapters 3, 4 and 5. As soon as you have determined a starting point, go to the relevant chapter, read the background and make a start.

Remember, wherever possible, to discuss your developmental needs with a colleague, college tutor or class teacher-mentor.

Needs analysis table J

Theme: Developing children's ability to make connections and solve problems
Area of development: ICT as a subject in its own right
Link to QTS Standards: QTS Standards 2002, para. 2.1 b

Getting Started	Date/Evidence	Developing Skills	Date/Evidence	Extending Skills	Date/Evidence
I have asked children about the uses of computer in the outside world.		I have begun to use presentation software more widely in my teaching.		I have looked at websites – created by schools and children – with children and evaluated them.	
I have begun to plan for writing with the computer and have considered the issues around this.		When children have produced writing I have begun to look at ways of publishing it with ICT.		I have talked with children about how work is presented for a range of audiences.	
On outings I have pointed out instances of computer use in other settings.		I have used either presentation software or desktop publishing with children.		I have talked with children about how to plan to write in a non-linear way.	
I have provided books and other resources about computers in the outside world and have visited websites to support this.		I have used presentation software and/or desktop publishing software as a means of teaching about ICT and its capacity to combine different sorts of files.		I have created a small number of linked webpages and resources with children.	
*If one or more of these is not yet ticked, you may find it helpful to complete the activities in 'Getting Started' on **pages 71–72**.*		*If one or more of these is not yet ticked, you may find it helpful to complete the activities in 'Developing your Skills' on **pages 106–108**.*		*If one or more of these is not yet ticked, you may find it helpful to complete the activities in 'Extending your Skills' on **pages 137–139**.*	

Guidance and needs assessment
⮕ Conclusion

Having used the needs analysis in each theme in this chapter, you should be able to plan your learning effectively based around the activities which follow in each of the three chapters: Chapter 3: Getting Started, Chapter 4: Developing your Skills and Chapter 5: Extending your Skills.

The table below summarises the activities and their locations in each of Chapters 3, 4 and 5. You could use this table to locate each of your starting points in each of the different themes.

THEMES	Getting Started	Developing your Skills	Extending your Skills
ICT in planning and assessment	**Word processing** and basic file management.	Using more advanced features in word processing	Collecting and making use of data and information from websites
ICT in locating and using resources, including for SEN and EAL	Observing the setting for ICT in a school	Finding out more about school provision/ interviewing the ICT co-ordinator	Exploring additional provision for children with SEN and EAL
Routine maintenance and connecting external equipment	Learning about the computer	Learning about the computer continued – basic troubleshooting and maintenance	Learning about peripheral devices for capturing and storing images
Using the Internet (becoming part of an online community for education)	Learning about the contribution of the Internet to education: sending and receiving **email**, using a **Web browser**	Organising a Web browser, searching and finding useful and usable resources for education	Joining an online community for education
Using ICT in curriculum subjects and in the learning areas of the Foundation Stage	Observing children and adults using the computer in subjects and learning areas across a range of software types	Subject related examples: using **databases** and **spreadsheets** in maths and science	Using ICT in the foundation subjects
Evaluating ICT resources (software, hardware, websites)	Reviewing educational software	Evaluating the use of a specific learning tool (curriculum example – floor robot)	Evaluating Internet resources/being aware of safety issues
Making the connections between subject schemes and plans	Listing available software and making links with subject areas/thinking about ICT in the Foundation Stage	Planning work in the schemes and strategies: literacy and numeracy	Combining different subject areas with ICT/using ICT in the Learning Areas of the Foundation Stage
Progression, continuity and issues of assessment in ICT	Introducing the scheme of work for ICT/ ICT in the Foundation Stage	Beginning to assess children's skills in ICT	Issues of continuity and progression
Developing children's ICT concepts and skills	Managing ICT in a range of settings	Involving children in the choice and use of a range of ICT tools	Evaluating teaching and learning with ICT
Developing children's ability to make connections and solve problems	Discussing real and work related examples of ICT with children	Integrating tasks and integrating skills with **presentation** software and desktop publishing	Using webpage authoring or hypermedia with children

A note on advice and assessment

The activities in the book should be used in conjunction with advice from the following people, as appropriate and as applicable:

⮕ your college based tutor;
⮕ your class teacher-mentor;
⮕ your school-based tutor;
⮕ your colleagues in your study group.

The needs analysis, in particular, would benefit from the contribution of some or all of these people, so that the activities which you undertake are of maximum benefit to you in your development as a teacher.

As you complete each activity, involve your tutors and colleagues in assessing whether you have completed them successfully and discussing what you may have learned in each case.

Chapter 3   **Getting Started** ⮑ Introduction

Contents

The activities in this section are aimed at people who are at the beginning of learning how to use ICT in their personal and professional development, in subject teaching and as a subject in its own right.

The work described can be carried out in a range of settings. You may have access to your own computer or to a computer in a college or a library in which you can carry out activities relating to personal and professional development. Most of this strand of development can be carried out at your own pace, in your own time.

The work described in the strands of ICT in subject teaching and ICT as a subject in its own right should be carried out in school with access to appropriate hardware and software and, on occasion, to appropriate Internet connections. We have already discussed the differing levels of resource provision across the country and how to access information about it. The situation with resources has changed completely during the past three or four years and most schools are much better resourced for ICT. There will, inevitably, be exceptions to this and not all of the activities in the sections on ICT in subject teaching and ICT as a subject in its own right can be carried out in school. There are occasions when it may be possible or even desirable to do these activities at home or college. One example would be when reviewing software or websites. In order to help you make a judgement about where each activity may or may not be most suitably carried out, each activity description contains a series of hints which suggest where it could be carried out.

For the purposes of auditing your development during your training, each strand of development is linked to a Standard in the DfES/TTA Qualifying to Teach booklet. As you complete each piece of evidence you can ask a mentor or visiting tutor to sign to say that this has been achieved. It can be added to your profiling. Each training provider will approach this in different ways and it is important to link completion of the tasks in this book to the profiling requirements of your own particular training course whether it is a college-based degree, PGCE or a Graduate Training Programme (GTP).

The activities in this chapter are arranged as follows:

Themes	Page reference	Activity title	Area of development
ICT in planning and in assessment	Page 45	**Word processing** and basic file management.	PERSONAL AND PROFESSIONAL USE OF ICT. (cf QTS standards 2002, para 2.5)
ICT in locating and using resources, including for SEN and EAL	Page 49	Observing the setting for ICT in a school.	
Routine maintenance and connecting external equipment	Page 53	Learning about the computer	
Using the Internet (Becoming part of an online community for education)	Page 55	Learning about the contribution of the Internet to education: sending and receiving **email**, using a **Web browser**	
Using ICT in curriculum subjects and in the learning areas of the Foundation Stage	Page 60	Observing children and adults using the computer in subjects and learning areas across a range of software types	ICT IN SUBJECT TEACHING. (cf QTS standards 2002, para. 3.3.10)
Evaluating ICT resources (software, hardware, websites)	Page 62	Reviewing educational software	
Making the connections between subject schemes and plans	Page 65	Listing available software and making links with subject areas/thinking about ICT in the Foundation Stage	
Progression, continuity and issues of assessment in ICT	Page 67	Introducing the scheme of work for ICT/ICT in the Foundation Stage	ICT AS A SUBJECT IN ITS OWN RIGHT. (cf QTS standards 2002, para. 2.1 b)
Developing children's ICT concepts and skills	Page 69	Managing ICT in a range of settings	
Developing children's ability to make connections and solve problems	Page 71	Discussing real and work-related examples of ICT with children	

Each activity is outlined in full and has the following information provided with it:

⊃ a link with the ICT National Curriculum and/or the QCA Scheme of work for ICT (if applicable);
⊃ a link to another subject in the National Curriculum or to its related strategies (for this example, where relevant);
⊃ QTS skills test link (if applicable);
⊃ a note of the possible Audit point against the Standards as set out in 'Qualifying to teach' (DFES/TTA, 2002);
⊃ some essential background to the activity, including such items as which equipment to use and which setting might be most appropriate for carrying it out;
⊃ a description of the activity and all the elements which go to make it up;
⊃ some ideas on how to evaluate its success.

Finally, each activity has some suggested background reading, either paper-based or on the Internet.

Link to
Professional
Standards for
QTS

Paragraph 2.5:

*'Those awarded Qualified Teacher Status must demonstrate [that] they know
how to use ICT effectively, both to teach their subject and to support their wider
professional role.'*

**Essential
background**

File management
Files are anything that the computer creates or collects that you decide to save.
These files you make or collect and save could be any or all of the following (or
others – feel free to add to the list!):

- ➲ a piece of writing;
- ➲ a video clip;
- ➲ an image;
- ➲ an address book;
- ➲ a piece of music;
- ➲ a page from the Internet.

Essentially, they are all pieces of stored digital information. The software you have
on your computer allows you to make them or to see them, hear them and use
them.

A word processing programme makes or reads a word processor file. Your
spreadsheet programme, in which you may monitor your finances, makes or reads
a spreadsheet file. Your digital camera takes image files and your computer's image
software allows you to see it. Your digital camera takes a clip which, if you have the
necessary hardware and software, your computer allows you to view and edit.

Making the files visible
Organisation of work on the computer depends on being able to see what's
going on. We know when a desk or workplace is untidy because we can see (or
not!) everything in front of us. When we are at work in a piece of writing at the
computer, it is not immediately obvious where all our work is. We see the writing
we are constructing, but we can't see other work we carried out earlier.

The first step is really to know how to view all the work on your computer and
where you go to see that on a regular basis. The next step is to create places to keep
all of the pieces of work you create or collect and to give those places meaningful
names. If you know how to do this, and if you do it regularly, you won't lose
anything and you will find your use of the computer, including the learning of other
pieces of software, much easier.

Organising the files
Some computers now have systems for suggesting ways in which you could organise
your work. The files that you make or collect or receive from elsewhere are all
stored in folders. The moment you learn how to make folders (and folders within
folders) is the moment you start to take control of your computer.

Windows users on PCs already have a folder already set up called 'My Documents'.
Some versions of Windows have other folders called, for example, 'My Music' or 'My
Pictures'. Apple computers have similar organisational suggestions for your work.
You could use these folders as suggested by your computer and you could refine

and develop them. You could also make your own folders, labelled in the way that means something to you. Either way, in order to take control of the way in which your computer is organised, you are going to have to learn how to make and label folders of your own.

Some of the things you might want to create and file during your teacher training include the following:

- notes;
- lesson plans;
- useful resources;
- assignments;
- images;
- video clips.

Within each of these you may wish to have a subject area or a topic. Each of these could be the heading of a folder. This activity begins by suggesting that before you do anything else you make some folders which are going to be of use to you.

The second part of the activity is to learn how to start up your word processor, make a file, make some changes to it and save it in the folder you have just made.

These activities can be carried out at home or in school or wherever you have access to a computer which is used regularly by you.

File management task

Go to the desktop of your computer. This is the opening screen where all the icons which allow you to organise the computer reside. It is the first screen you see once your computer has finished loading all of the software and start-up files it needs.

On a Windows PC computer, double-click the left mouse button on the icon labelled My Computer. This should open a window which gives you a map of your computer. There are some conventions you need to be aware of at this stage.

If you see anything labelled A: this is the floppy disk drive. If you put a disk in the drive and double click on A: you will open a window which gives you a map of what is on the disk. It will show you the all of the files on it.

To go back to the view which showed you the whole of your computer, you can either click on the word 'Back' if you see it, or on the word 'Up' which is written underneath a folder with an 'Up' arrow on it.

You should see a small flat grey icon next to a letter C:. This is the hard disk inside your computer which stores all of your program files and work. If you double click on it you are likely to see many folders in a long list running down the screen. Double click on the icon for a folder called 'My Documents'. This is a good place to start organising things. Notice that there is an Address line shown in the window which tells you where you are at all times. In the example shown, your address for that moment in time is C:\My Documents

Along the top line above the window, you will see the word File. Click on it and then on the word New ... Both of these clicks are with the left mouse button. This is the button with which you make choices on a PC in Windows. One of the choices you can make at this point is to make a new folder. Click on Folder, which should be at the top of a list of choices. A new folder will then appear which bears the words New Folder highlighted in blue, type in the name of your choice. The suggestion here, as a practice, is to create a folder called 'Notes'.

Figure 3.1 is a flow diagram of the procedure for a PC running a version of Windows.

One of the views possible on a Windows PC, showing your 'My Documents' folder.
Windows is regularly updated and comes in many different forms, all of which allow you to customise your view. This illustrates a classic Windows 98 view. Windows 2000 and Windows XP which come later look very similar. Earlier versions (Windows 95 for example) do not have the address bar.

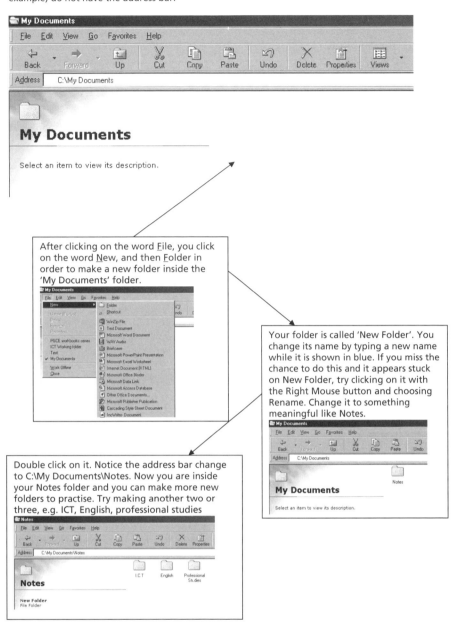

Fig. 3.1 Making folders on a PC.

On an Apple Mac, the procedure is similar. To see a map of the files and folders on your computer's hard disk, double click on the grey icon which is labelled Macintosh HD (meaning Macintosh Hard Disk). You can make new folders in this area and label them. As on the PC, you can make folders inside folders inside folders.

Word processing task

Your PC or your Apple Mac will have a word processor on it somewhere. You are probably aware that the predominant word processing software is called 'Word' for the PC and is part of a suite of programmes called Microsoft Office. There are now many versions of this software published with new variants coming on the market all the time. There is also a version of Microsoft Office for the Apple Mac computer. For those without Office, Microsoft also have a cut-down version called 'Works' and Mac users have 'Apple Works'. Whatever your situation, with a little hunting around you will find a word processor somewhere on your system and you will be able to launch it by double clicking on its icon. On the PC, this is usually a 'W' in blue somewhere on your screen. If you don't see it, click on the word 'Start' on the bottom left and then 'Programs' and have a hunt for the Microsoft Word program On the Apple Mac you can use the Finder on the top right of the screen to look at the program you are currently using or find another one.

Having launched the software, all this activity requires you to do is to type in a few lines of text in note form. And then to save it in your Notes folder which you created.

Evaluation and follow-up

Because of the impossibility of providing a bespoke guide for every user of every different possible computer, there are certain generic characteristics of the activity which you have to consider when evaluating its success. If the instructions above did not apply to your situation or completely match your computer, what did you have to do to overcome it? What were the places you had to go to discover how to do the following:

1 Make a folder on your hard drive and label it
2 Make some folders inside that folder and name them (making at least 3)
3 Launch a Word Processor of some description
4 Type a small file and then save it in the folder you created earlier

Reflect and make any notes that help you in the table below as memory joggers:

Activity	Notes on how to do it on your computer (memory joggers)
Making a new folder on the computer, labelling it and making new folders inside it	
Opening a word processor, creating a short file and saving it in a folder I've made	

A note on attitude

Computers make many people feel inadequate. You will know people who say things like, *'This always happens to me when I sit down in front of the computer'* or *'Computers don't like me,'* or *'I always break computers'*. Maybe you feel that way too. It will be helpful at this point to develop a more robust attitude. You are an intelligent person, undertaking demanding training in a demanding profession. You may already have a degree. You may already be managing difficult logistical situations (such as parenthood and teacher training). Provided that you approach the computer in a positive and logical way and give it the time you need, you will succeed.

If it helps, you might want to start blaming the computer more often. Why does the market leading operating system (Windows) require you to press 'Start' in order to Shut Down correctly? Is this a logical sequence of events? How will you explain it to children?

Why, if a PC crashes, does it come back to life with a blue screen which proceeds to blame you (Because windows was not shut down properly etc. etc.)?

There are things that you have to remember to do and there are precautions that you need to take, but a great deal of what appears to go wrong is not necessarily your fault.

Finally, if a computer or piece of software is not easy to use by an intelligent person, such as yourself, at this point in time, why isn't it?

If you feel that the activity has been beyond you and you require a different starting point or an easier, gentler approach to getting started, there are some places to go for help (see Bibliography at the end of this book). These sorts of book might provide you with a starting point. Some of the titles insult your intelligence slightly, but be aware that the content is often much more useful than the cover would suggest.

Finally, if you feel that you have successfully completed the task, return to the needs analysis table and mark it off with the date. Ask your mentor or tutor about being able to use this activity as evidence of meeting the Standards for QTS. Then, move on to another activity.

ICT in locating and using resources

Link to Professional Standards for QTS

Paragraph 2.5

'Those awarded Qualified Teacher Status must demonstrate (that) they know how to use ICT effectively, both to teach their subject and to support their wider professional role.'

Essential background

This area of learning is all about being able to identify and evaluate useful ICT resources of all kinds.

A starting point, represented by this activity is to have a look at what is available in a placement school or, if you are on a GTP course, the workplace in which you are being trained.

If you haven't seen ICT in school since you were at school yourself you might be surprised at the range of provision. On the other hand, you may have some of your lower expectations confirmed. ICT equipment alone is only part of the story and the government does recognise, in some initiatives, the importance of the human beings maintaining and teaching with it.

It is worth noting that there is not uniformly good provision of ICT equipment across the country and trying to look briefly at some of the reasons why. Knowing about why your school does or does not have the facilities you and the children need to use ICT in subject teaching and as a subject in its own right can prevent you from blaming the wrong people or from feeling dis-empowered.

The position of ICT in schools has changed beyond recognition since the government introduced massive spending in the form of the 'National Grid for Learning' (henceforth NGfL). At the time of writing, in the spring of 2002, there has been, since 1998, a spending of about £1.6 bn in the various constituent parts of the initiative known as the NGfL. Whilst equipment, as noted above, is only part of the story it is a fact that without certain minimum levels of provision, you cannot teach with ICT.

The DfES collects statistics on ICT in schools every year and you can obtain this information annually, every October. In the activity on **pages 113–114**, we will look at how to go about this and the collection of other statistics which will be useful to you as a teacher. In the meantime, it is useful to look at the basic figures on computer numbers in school.

The table below compares the most recent available statistics on computers in primary school with those of the figures for 1998. As you will see, there have been great changes taking place:

Item	Figures for 1998	Figures for 2001
Average number of computers per school	13.3	20.7
Average number of pupils per computer	17.6	11.8
Percentage of schools connected to the Internet	17	96

Source: DfES (2001) *Statistics of Education: Survey of Information and Communications Technology in Schools 2001* (Issue no. 09/01) p.8

Perhaps the figure which will surprise you most is the number of schools with Internet connections. 96% of primary schools as of October 2001 were connected to the Internet. Many activities in this book reflect the sea change which this has brought about. However, not all connections at the moment are fast, cheap, distributed across the school and providing the revolution in curriculum delivery which has been envisaged by the government (see the original paper which launched the NGfL – DfEE (1997) *Connecting the Learning Society*).

There are equal numbers of caveats connected to the figure which show huge numbers of computers in schools compared to 1998. These figures reflect national averages for schools who returned the survey questionnaires. They assume that only computers which are less than five years old are counted. They do not reveal much about the differences which exist between schools and between LEAs. In order to access the money on behalf of their schools, LEAs were required to write bids containing plans for implementation. LEAs who were already well advanced, comfortable with these concepts (perhaps having active ICT advisory teams) and, finally, good at writing bids, were successful in getting early funding and beginning to build an infrastructure.

Similarly at school level, many LEAs required schools to put in place development plans before they could bid for new hardware and Internet access. For schools with a well supported and well organised ICT co-ordinator and/or sympathetic head and governing body this was not a problem. Such schools were usually successful in gaining ICT resources. Schools without these advantages (at the time of asking) sometimes suffered.

Your school could be in one of three broad categories of resource. It could be a low resource, medium resource or high resource setting. The table below (adapted from Sharp, Potter *et al.*, 2000) offers some definitions of these terms:

High-resource setting:
Network room, printing – sometimes in colour – is available at every station.
Internet connection is cheap and quick, via an ADSL broadband connection or better and moderated by an LEA.
There is a technician who regularly comes to repair computers, change cartridges, load to new software etc.
Appropriate software is available for every age phase.
There are also stations connected to the network available in the classroom to carry on with work begun in the network room.
The school is implementing a cohesive strategy with high levels of LEA support.

Medium-resource setting:
A working computer and printer in every classroom.
An Internet connection somewhere in school OR a network room with computers removed from classrooms and placed there to capitalise on resources.
Some programmable toys are available.
Repairs are dealt with fairly promptly.
A scheme of work is being implemented.
The school has a plan.
There is a sense that ICT is valued and that within the next two or three years the school will move forward and become a high-resource setting.

Low-resource setting:
An older, frequently broken computer in the classroom or one between two.
A shared printer.
Low staff morale, low spending on ICT, no ICT co-ordinator, no technician.
Frequent sightings of batik and plant pots placed over computers.
No scheme of work in place.
No ink cartridges or ribbons in the printers.
Poor software titles with children from Year 1 to Year 6 doing the same thing on the computer (copy typing, doodling in a Paint package or playing a number game).
At the present time, this school is not providing the entitlement to ICT for its children. Such a school would find OFSTED and the LEA asking them to make changes urgently.

Most schools are somewhere on a continuum between the high resource setting and the low resource setting. This activity requires that you investigate provision at a surface level initially and see if you can estimate how this will affect your ability to deliver skills in ICT in Subject Teaching and ICT as a subject in its own right.

Task

This activity must be carried out in school. Record information about the surface features of the ICT in school. As noted above, the task at this stage is to record what hardware appears to be available for use. Later observational tasks will require looking at the software available as well as at what is actually going on in terms of teaching and learning.

Use the following questions about typical resources in school to guide you:

⮕ Do you find that there are computers in all the classrooms?

⮕ Are they all in a network room?

⮕ Are they in a room all together but not connected to each other?

⮕ Are they all the same type? That is, are they PC? Or AppleMac (perhaps the newer iMac computers?) Or Acorn? Or older RM Nimbus 186s?

⮕ Are they all roughly the same age?

⮕ Which classes seem to have the older equipment?

⮕ Are there any working printers? For example:

inkjet printers, colour or black and white;

laser printers, as above;

older dot matrix printers.

⮕ Are there any portable computers for you and the children to use?

Acorn Pocketbooks, I or II or III (which are the same as Psion Organisers series 3)

Apple e-Mates

Laptops from Acorn or Apple or RM

Multimedia laptops from a pilot project

Dreamwriters

AlphaSmarts

Others?

⮕ Is there equipment for supporting access to ICT for children with Special Educational Needs?

⮕ For example, are there Concept Keyboards, Touch Windows, Large Keyboards, Smaller or Larger mice?

⮕ Is there anything else in use for specific children?

⮕ Is there Internet access for you and the children? If so, what kind is it?

via a modem (external or internal) of varying speed and quality;

or via an ISDN line;

or via cable;

or via a local authority or higher education Internet connection.

⮕ How fast does it appear to be?

⮕ Where is it available? For example:

on one computer in the library;

on three computers linked together;

in the network room;

in the network room and in the whole school in every class;

any other variation.

⮕ Is there a large training monitor or an Interactive whiteboard so that all children can see the screen when you are talking to the whole class about the ICT activity? Has a large TV been connected via an adapter for this purpose?

⮕ Are there programmable toys for you to use with children (you will have a go in future activities)? For example:

a Roamer, Pixie, Pip;

a Valiant turtle (infra red linked to an Acorn usually);

a Jessops turtle (linked by cable).

⮕ Are there any Digital cameras?

⮕ Do you have to connect them to a computer to download the pictures?

⮕ Do they shoot straight to a disk?

⮕ Do you have access to a video camera?

⮕ Is there any way you can download the video clips?

⮕ Has the school got access, for example, to an iBook and digital video camera?

⮕ Have you and the children got access to a scanner somewhere?

Hand scanners

Flatbed scanners

⮕ Are there any electronic keyboards?

⮕ Can you record into a computer using MIDI equipment?

⮕ Is there a microphone for recording speech in multimedia presentations or music making?

⮕ Do you have access to the range of non-computer ICT equipment that you need to support your subject teaching:

tape recorders

video recorders

CD players?

Evaluation and follow-up

The success of the activity is in actually carrying it out in some detail. By the end of it, you should know about the kinds of hardware and Internet connection. You will also have picked up on the level of support for ICT in the school as a whole. This knowledge will be deepened in further activities at a later stage which look more closely at what the teachers and learners are doing with what is available to them.

There is more on the background to this in:

Sharp, J, Potter, J, Allen, A and Loveless, A (2002) *Primary ICT: Knowledge, Understanding & Practice.* Exeter: Learning Matters.

Further detail on the statistical analysis of computers in schools is available in the most recent bulletin:

DfES (2001) *Statistics of Education: Survey of Information and Communications Technology in Schools 2001* (Issue no. 09/01). London: DfES.

A survey of the history of ICT in schools up to about the time of the NGfL is contained in:

McFarlane, A (ed.) (1997) *Information Technology and Authentic Learning.* London: Routledge, Chapter 1.

The background to the huge amount of government spending in the UK since 1998 is contained in the following:

DfEE (1997) *Connecting the Learning Society.* London: DfEE.

If you feel you have successfully completed the task, return to the development matrix and mark it off with the date. Ask your mentor or tutor about being able to use this activity as evidence of meeting the Standards for QTS.

Chapter 3   Routine maintenance and connecting equipment

Link to Professional Standards for QTS

Paragraph 2.5:

'Those awarded Qualified Teacher Status must demonstrate (that) they know how to use ICT effectively, both to teach their subject and to support their wider professional role.'

Essential background

As noted previously, you could find yourself working in any one of a range of possible settings. You could also find yourself working in a school with any one of a range of computers. The following activity is all about familiarising yourself with the computer or workstation you are mostly going to be working with in this particular school placement. It is something you could carry out again, when and if you move schools.

The activity has been designed with a non-expert in mind. Partly it is simply an exploration in your own time of some of the issues raised. Partly it is a chance to discover even more about the computers in your school. Parts of it could be carried out at home but the greatest benefit would be derived from getting to know the computer or network suite you will be using with children in school.

Task

This activity takes the form of an investigation into the computer which you are using with the children. If you are using a network computer, look at any of the workstations.

Establish the make and type of computer which you are going to investigate. If at all possible, look at the connections at the rear of the machine. Are there any manuals or other materials to help you work out what the various connections are?

Whether the computer you are looking at is a PC or an iMac or an Acorn, there are many connections in common. Laptops tend to have some different sorts of slots and connections. It would be very difficult to list them all, but try to look for the following:

⮕ A power connector, usually in the form of what is called a 'kettle lead' because it looks like the kind of lead used with an electric kettle.
⮕ Sometimes there is an extra power port used to take power to the monitor. Nowadays, many computers have separate power cables going into their monitors.
⮕ Two small round connectors in sockets nearby to one another, usually helpfully labelled with a keyboard and mouse respectively. Sometimes these are, even more helpfully, colour coded.
⮕ A set of sockets and connectors in a strip, also labelled which resemble small headphone sockets. These are the audio connectors for sound going into or coming out of the computer. They will be labelled with speaker out signs, line in (for audio going in), and microphone sockets.
⮕ A parallel port, used to connect a printer normally on a standalone computer. The connector for this port comprises a set of 25 pins arranged in two parallel rows (one of 13 and one of 12).
⮕ A serial port, used to connect peripheral devices such as modems, some scanners, some personal organisers etc. The connector which fits this port usually consists of 9 pins arranged in two parallel rows (one of 5 and one of 4).
⮕ A USB port, used to connect printers, scanners, digital cameras – almost any device you can think of. It has become a standard way of connecting in recent years and is set to replace the parallel and serial ports as a way of connecting devices. Many computers now have more than one. They look small and flat with no visible pins.

➲ An SVGA or video-out port, used to connect the monitor. This is similar to the serial port in appearance but contains more sockets arranged in three rows of 5, usually arranged so that middle row is out of alignment with the two above and below. It is not possible to mistakenly plug a serial device into this, although the sockets are superficially similar.

➲ A network card connector, also known as an RS 45 connector. This looks a little bit like a telephone connector and socket.

➲ A modem connector, which looks exactly like a telephone connector only smaller than the part that goes into the wall. This will only be seen if the computer has a built in modem.

➲ A Firewire or Video in port which is very small in appearance, rectangular in cross section, used to connect to digital video cameras. All iMacs have these and many PCs are now being sold with them as standard.

Complete the following table:

Questions	Answers in the form of notes to use as an aide memoire
What kind of computer am I using?	
Is it standalone or on a network?	
If standalone, which ports are present on the computer and what devices are connected to them (if any)? Choose one or more from: Power Parallel Serial USB Network Modem Monitor And any others from the list in the text above	
How do I switch on?	
How do I log on (if applicable i.e if on a network)?	
How do the children log on?	
Which printer or printers are available?	
Is there a CD or DVD drive available?	
Do I know how to log off?	

Evaluation and follow-up

Were you able to complete the sections on the connectors at the back of the computer? Were you able to say how you would complete some basic troubleshooting? If the answer to both of these questions is yes then the activity has been successful. It may be that the situation is more complex for you and that the activity can only be partly successful because all technical difficulties are ultimately dealt with by other adults in the school. The answer is to do only what you can in this area and remember that it is an area which is important to develop in the future.

There are many self-help books which allow you to develop some basic troubleshooting skills. There are also websites which explain about the basics of computers and their connections (PC and Mac and Acorn). Some helpful ones include:

www.howstuffworks.com

This link takes you straight to the computer section:

www.howstuffworks.com/category.htm?cat=Comp

If you feel you have successfully completed the task, return to the needs analysis table and mark it off with the date. Ask your mentor or tutor about being able to use this activity as evidence of meeting the Standards for QTS.

Chapter 3 — Becoming part of an online community for education

Link to Professional Standards for QTS

Paragraph 2.5

'Those awarded Qualified Teacher Status must demonstrate (that) they know how to use ICT effectively, both to teach their subject and to support their wider professional role.'

Essential background

This activity introduces you to two pieces of software which are most frequently used when someone is engaging in use of the Internet, namely, a web browser and email.

In whatever way you connect, once you have connected you can click on the icon for your web browser, the piece of software which allows you to see web pages and find other web pages. The three most common web browsers are Internet Explorer (whose icon is a blue e), Netscape (whose icon is a white N on a blue background, or a ship's navigator's wheel) or Opera (whose icon is a red O). If you are connecting to the Internet with America Online (AOL) as your service provider, you will have your own web browser provided.

The web browser
The web browser displays pages for you to use which may contain any of the following: text, images, links to videos, audio files, animations and so on. These pages have all been set up or 'marked up' in the same way using a 'behind the scenes' language, a kind of code which the browser then interprets and displays for you. This code is called HTML, hypertext markup language. Do you need to know this? In some ways, yes, because files which are written in HTML do behave differently from normal files. As you look at a web page you will see that some piece of text are in different colours or underlined. These pieces of text are more than ordinary text, they are a 'hypertext' link to another file or to another part of the page.

The pages you see or look for could be on any computer anywhere in the world. Each page that is held on the computer connected to the Internet has a unique address. You will have seen these addresses all over the place on advertising hoardings or magazines or food wrappers because companies which make all these products have pages set up on the Internet. They usually begin with www. They are usually lowercase (because that is the way that some operating systems of the big computers on the Internet prefer it) and contain no spaces. They must be typed accurately or you will not find the page you are looking for.

Figure 3.2 on the next page shows how a web page is displayed on a web browser and labels the main features of it. You will see that the example is of the homepage of the National Grid for Learning, a useful starting point for you as a teacher looking for pages which are relevant to education and contain useful links to further resources.

You will see in one of the captions how to use the web browser to store addresses of regularly visited sites to which you know you will return (thereby avoiding any need to remember those occasionally frustrating and arcane website addresses).

We will look in much more depth at how to obtain resources for teaching and learning from the Internet in future activities in this and the other two learning areas.

This is the address bar where you would type the web address of the page you are looking for. You can see that this web browser is at the opening page of the National Grid for Learning web page www.ngfl.gov.uk

This is the main page, displayed with images. As you move the mouse over some of the different coloured text or the contents list on the left, the mouse changes to a pointing finger. The web browser has detected that the piece of text represents a hyperlink to another file or another part of this file.

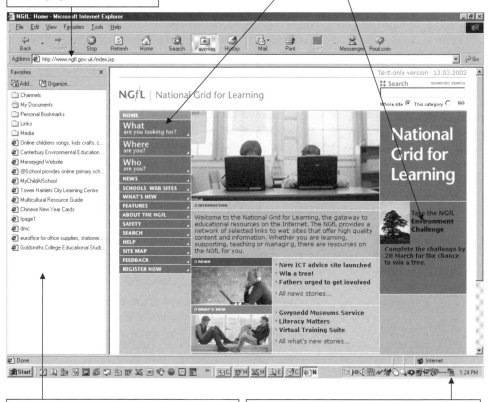

This web browser, called Internet Explorer allows you to store web pages that you know you will visit frequently. They are stored as 'Favorites' (sic). You can have them set up to be displayed all the time (as in this case) or hidden until you need them. Clicking on 'Add to favorites' adds the page you are currently viewing to the list. The next time you start Internet Explorer you just click on the link to the appropriate site in the Favorites. You do not need to type the address in the Address Bar. Netscape calls these Bookmarks. It is the same concept.

One other thing to notice is that this computer was connected over a modem link. You can see the two green computer icons in the bottom right next to the time display. To disconnect a computer connected in this way, double click on it and click on 'Disconnect'.

Fig. 3.2 Web browser window.

Email

Along with the ability to display information and retrieve it over great distance comes the ability to send messages to people who are connected to the Internet. For this, you use a different piece of software – an email reader. Some of the most common are Outlook, Netscape Mail and so on.

An email address is like a pigeonhole into which messages are sorted on arrival from anywhere on the Internet. When you connect to your Internet Service Provider, you launch your email and, having gained access to your pigeonhole by entering your username and password, you collect your messages. They appear in an onscreen display known as your 'inbox'. Some of this process is automated on some computers so that you may not even be aware that you are entering a username and password or asking to see your 'inbox'. It may all have been set up for you.

When someone writes an email to you they must address it to your username and then say 'at' which computer your email can be found. This where the 'at' sign, @, comes into the equation. Email addresses are you@your-internet-service-provider.co.uk or similar. Internet service providers are so many and so varied and contain different stylised addresses. You may be with 'aol', so your address would be your-username@aol.com. You may be with 'virgin' so that your email address looks something like your-username@virgin.net You may have a college email address, so your email would be you@collegename.ac.uk Notice that the end of the address, just as for web pages, gives away the kind of account. The '.ac.uk' indicates that the user has an account at a college.

Web-based email

All of the email described above is collected at the computer or in the network area on which the Internet account is held. It is stored on the local computer or in your network area at college. However, some of these service providers have web based access to your email account so that you can read email from any computer which is connected to the Internet.

Some users prefer to have an email address which is always independent from the computer on which they usually access the Internet. In other words, they want to have an email account which they can access from any computer which is connected to the Internet at any time. These addresses are enormously flexible because of this. You can read your email at your own computer, in a library, in an Internet café, while on holiday or anywhere you can connect to the Internet. The two most popular versions of these are hotmail accounts and yahoo accounts. There are many others. In order to make the accounts you will need to visit either company's web page (www.hotmail.com and/or www.yahoo.co.uk) and follow the instructions on how to make an account.

Having such an address will be of enormous use to you in your training year or years, because you can access your email at home, at college, at school. You may move from place to place but your email stays the same. If you have more than one email address, you can arrange for it all to be forwarded to one place and read it all there. As with all things to do with ICT there is much to be gained by being pro-active, discovering these facilities and making use of them.

Figure 3.3 shows the main features of an email composition window.

> This shows a message composition window popping up in front of the main Inbox in Outlook – one commonly used email programme.

> You address the message where it says 'To...' and you write a subject for the message where it says 'Subject'.
> When you are ready, you click 'Send' to send it.

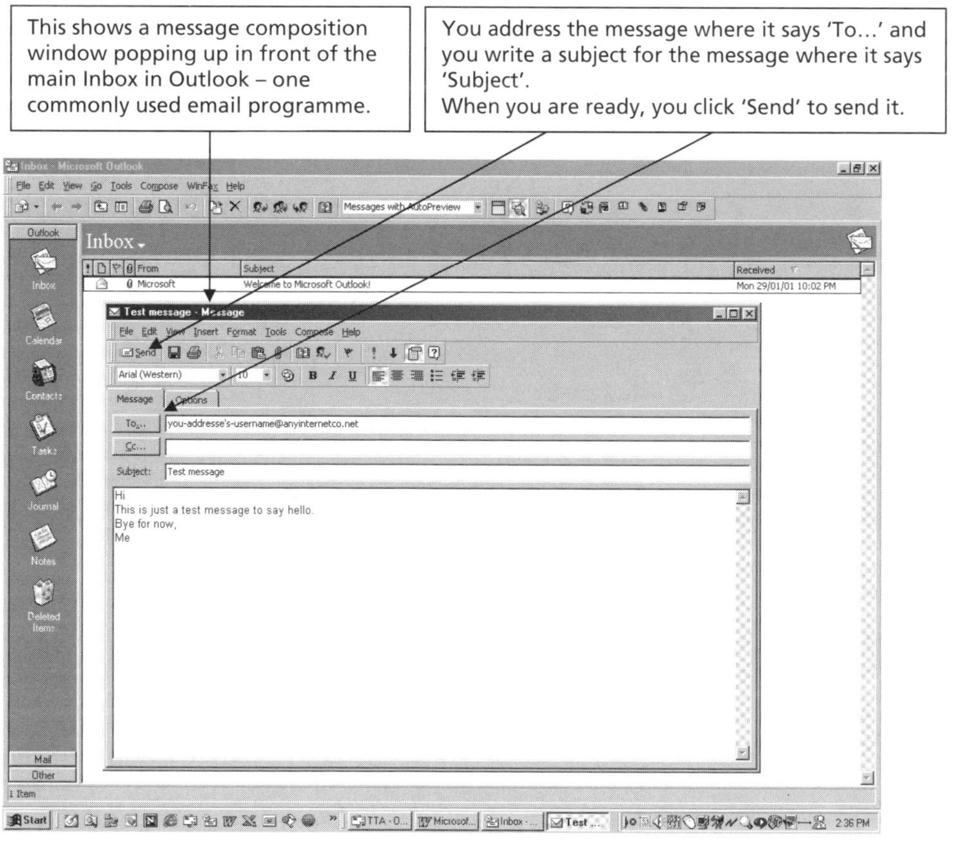

Fig. 3.3   The basics of composing an email in Outlook.

When you are reading email from other people, you see all the messages you have in your 'Inbox'. When you want to read one, double click on it to open it. A slightly different window to the one above opens, with different choices in the top line – to reply, forward etc. Clicking on Reply opens an email composition window with your new message already addressed in it.

If all of this sounds confusing, it isn't. It is harder to read and write about than actually do. Sending and receiving email is one of the easiest activities at the computer. All of the analogies onscreen to office life and to posting, memos etc. are very helpful.

Sometimes, you need to send a much larger piece of work as an email. You might need to send a whole file, such as a Word document or an image file. In this case you compose a short message in the same way as usual (along the lines of 'Please see the attached file…'). Before you click on 'Send' you click on an 'Attach' command or, more usually, a paperclip icon (another analogy to the real world). In the window which appears, you will be invited to navigate to the file that you want to send. By now, you will see that, once again, we are returning to the importance of knowing where your files are. If you have been organised (see activity 1A) and created the folders you need and filed your work in them, you will be able to attach the file with ease.

When you receive attachments from someone else, they appear as a filename or a paperclip in your window. When you double-click on the file, it will open up in the appropriate software on your computer.

Please note that all of the popular email readers are capable of performing these functions. Whilst the descriptions apply to the Outlook mail reader, if you look closely along all of the possible menu items on the email software in front of you, you will find these commands and possibilities. They work with web-based email as well as installed email readers on your computer.

The following activities suggest that you simply get on a computer which is connected to the Internet and have a go. They can be carried out at any computer which you use which has access to the Internet – at home or at school or college.

Task 1: web browser
Double click on your web browser icon and type the following in to the address bar (see illustration above) www.ngfl.gov.uk

Next, visit any two of the further links e.g 'About the NGfL' and 'Schools web sites'. Use the button on the browser labelled Back to get back to the NGfL starting page (known as a home page in Internet jargon)

Make any relevant notes as memory joggers on how to do it. Add the NGFL and then at least two further pages to your list of 'Favourites'.

Shut down your web browser, re-start it and re-visit one of the web pages you have listed in your 'Favourites'.

Task 2: email
Open an email window on your computer and type in the address of someone you know who is connected to the Internet. Agree with them in advance that you will be doing this to test your knowledge of email. This person could be a colleague on the course or a family member (here, there or anywhere in the world). The important thing is to experience opening the new mail window (Click on New Mail) and writing and composing and sending a new message.

Ask them to reply and then immediately send a reply to them. This time, attach a small Word file (such as the one created in activity 1A or similar).

The next part of the activity is for you if you do not have your own computer, but you have access to one at school or college or in a library. If you have your own computer and would like to do it anyway, because you feel it would be useful to you during your training, then please do.

Visit the web pages for yahoo or hotmail (see addresses above or use any free web based email provider) and create an account. You will be asked to provide some details about yourself. You will also be asked to choose a username and password (think about this in advance and choose something you will remember; follow the onscreen instructions about numbers of characters allowed etc.). Finally, untick the boxes that say you would be happy to receive junk email (you wouldn't, believe me). Then distribute your address to your family, friends and college or school.

Evaluation and follow-up

Do you feel confident that you could start a web browser and view any page for which you previously had the address? (Note, we will be looking at searching in other activities).

Do you feel confident that you could send and receive a simple email from someone?

If not, repeat as often as you like and at your own pace. There is no hurry with any of this and you do not have to feel that you are an expert. Many of the best ways to learn are to have a context for what you are doing. The context for learning how to use either of these pieces of software and the Internet generally are provided by many of the future activities in the book.

Kennedy, A (2001) *The Rough Guide to the Internet.* London: Rough Guides.

Sharp, J, Potter, J, Allen, A and Loveless, A (2002) *Primary ICT: Knowledge, Understanding & Practice.* Exeter: Learning Matters, Section A Chapter 5 on the Internet.

As for the previous section, the Internet itself is a mine of information about the Internet and how it works, try www.howstuffworks.com

If you feel you have successfully completed the task, return to the needs analysis table and mark it off with the date. Ask your mentor or tutor about being able to use this activity as evidence of meeting the Standards for QTS.

Chapter 3 — Using ICT in curriculum subjects and in the Foundation Stage learning areas

Link to Professional Standards for QTS

Paragraph 3.3.10

'Those awarded Qualified Teacher Status must demonstrate (that) they use ICT effectively in their teaching.'

Essential background

Making observations of children working with each other and with adults using the computer requires you to take note of three major sorts of contextual information, namely the context of the:

1 resources available;
2 National Curriculum and the Curriculum for the Foundation Stage;
3 context of teaching and learning theory.

By the end of the activity you should have a greater understanding of teaching and learning with ICT. You should be able to see that, like any other subject or resource, it requires forward planning which takes note of the various contexts for it to succeed.

Before completing this activity, you must make sure you have read **pages 21–24** in Chapter 2 to gain an overall understanding of each of the contexts. The activities must be carried out in the company of real children working with computers in a school.

Preparation
Observe two children using the computer in subjects and learning areas across a range of software types

Task 1: The *resource* setting
If the children are working at a computer in the classroom, describe the resource. Where is it? How much time do they spend on it? Are they working alone, one after the other, or collaboratively? Listen to (record if possible) the dialogue around a particular issue.

In an ICT suite, apply the same criteria. If possible, make a comparison with the experience of ICT in a classroom.

Task 2: The *curriculum* setting
Is there a lesson plan? Which curriculum subject or learning area is described? Are the children operating in more than one area? Have they been given a particular task within the curriculum context? Describe it. Is it open ended or does it have a narrow focus? Are they working in a NLS or NNS session? How has the activity been integrated? If you are in the Foundation Stage, which of the learning areas is the focus? Does the activity have a basis in more than one learning area? Are they working without a curriculum context in an ICT lesson?

Task 3: The *teaching and learning*
Try to make some judgement about the thinking that has gone into the design of the activity. Are the children being asked to think about what they are doing? Are they using the computer as a tool? Are they using the computer to rehearse and revise knowledge as content rather than practise development of a skill? Describe the setting in these terms. What adult interactions are possible? Do they ask for help and what happens when they do? Are the children talking about the decisions they are making? What does this tell you about the quality of the learning experience?

Evaluation and follow-up

How easy was it for you to observe the setting?

Did you understand the curriculum context or did you need to know more?

When you were thinking about the teaching and learning issues, did you make connections with other learning areas?

Did the activity help you to understand more about the need for planning in ICT?

Crook, Charles (1996) *Computers and the Collaborative Experience of Learning.* London: Routledge.
Somekh, B and Davis, N (eds) (1997) *Using IT Effectively in Teaching and Learning.* London: Routledge.
Read about IMPACT2 on the BECTA website at www.becta.org.uk/research

If you feel you have successfully completed the task, return to the needs analysis table and mark it off with the date. Ask your mentor or tutor about being able to use this activity as evidence of meeting the Standards for QTS.

Chapter 3 Evaluating ICT resources

**Link to
Professional
Standards for
QTS**

Paragraph 3.3.10:

'Those awarded Qualified Teacher Status must demonstrate (that) they use ICT effectively in their teaching.'

**Essential
background**

As noted in Chapter 2, having benchmarks against which to judge educational software is essential when making both practical decisions about cost and pedagogical decisions about the way in which the software enhances teaching and learning.

In the first place, some broad categories are useful as a framework within which to begin making judgements. The TEEM website (see 'Guidance and Needs Assessment') and others use the following:

➲ Content rich resources – These are software titles with specific subject-related or reference content. Examples of content rich resources would include encyclopaedias, dictionaries, atlases and so on.
➲ Tools – These are sometimes known as 'Content free resources', although 'tools' is the preferred terminology. These are software titles which allow for tasks to be performed by the child. Examples would be word processors, spreadsheets, presentation software, multimedia software, iMovie and so on.
➲ Courseware – These are also known as tutorial software titles. These contain specific tutorial content to support a curriculum area. For younger children this might include aspects of phonics and reading. For older children this might include more complex grammatical work or work to support a particular science concept.
➲ Assessment software – These sorts of titles aim to support SATS and other forms of assessment.

It is worth mentioning another software category which you may encounter which is a combination of Courseware and Management/Assessment Software. This sort of software comes as part of an Integrated Learning System or ILS. These are sophisticated, usually networked packages which collect information about the children and then deliver targeted modules appropriate to the child's needs. An ILS can be closed or open. In the closed version the teacher has limited control over the units which are delivered to the child. She or he can view assessment data but the route through the course content and the areas visited are determined by the computer. In an Open ILS (OILS) the teacher has more control over the management and operation of the system and can, in some cases, add software titles and determine which areas of content are open to children.

Publishers of educational software provide the software on a license to schools which can be for one machine, or several, or for the whole school (a site licence). The software can be used on one machine in a classroom (standalone) or installed on a school network. The ICT co-ordinator at the school should have the details of this.

Some educational software is provided as part of a 'toolkit'. Increasingly, software suppliers wish to be seen as providing a one-stop solution to teachers looking for a child-friendly word processor, desktop publisher, database, web-page authoring or hypermedia tool. In some ways they are replicating the Microsoft Office approach. If you have previously been in an office environment, it might be helpful to think of a toolkit as a cut-down Office suite. You will find that there are additional areas being covered and some toolkits will stray into content rich areas.

In addition to TEEM as a source of reviews, the BESA (British Educational Software Association) is a useful source of contact details for software suppliers. The annual BETT show at Olympia (January) and the Education Show at the Birmingham NEC (March) are good places to find out about software for many curriculum areas and age phases. The BETT website (www.bettshow.com) also features a directory of software publishers and suppliers.

Software usually comes with support materials in paper form or via the Internet. It is worth including these in any evaluation. Could you turn to the support materials for help in finding classroom and curriculum applications for the software or does it begin and end with installation instructions?

When you look at the software, it is useful to try to judge the intended reading age of the user against the actual onscreen text. Is it accessible to its target audience. This might sound obvious, but some software is surprisingly wide of the mark and requires a lot of adult support and intervention to make it work.

When you judge the software in the final instance, you need to make some comments about its overall effectiveness. Would it be useful as a learning resource? If it was chosen as a content rich resource, would it make the material accessible and usable by the children or by you as a teacher? If it was being employed as a tool, would it allow the child to think creatively and independently at the same time as developing their subject knowledge? Does it allow the child to think actively or is the child passively consuming the content? These are important issues because one of the skills of working with ICT is to know when and how best to use it as a resource and when to use a different resource.

Issues of navigability and ease of use are important. Children should be able to use the software after some initial input from you but, in general, by themselves. Notes should be helpful, icons intuitive and saving and retrieval (where applicable) should be easily understood. Children should be able to follow a thread, to see what is coming up next and how to get there.

In 'Courseware' in particular, but also in some 'Content Rich Resources' explanations of concepts should be clear and unambiguous and supported by the onscreen environment and activities.

This first software review can be carried out at home or college or in school.

Preparation
Choose a software title which has been specifically designed to meet the needs of learners in the Foundation Stage (3–5), Key Stage 1 (5–7) or Key Stage 2 (8–11).

Task
Look at the following issues.

Basic Information:	
Name of the software title	
Publisher	
Supplier	
Web address for further info	
Computer platform(s)	
Network or standalone	
If standalone – Does it require the CD in drive?	
Can be installed to the hard drive?	

Software type (choose one):	
Content rich	
Tool	
Courseware	
Assessment	
ILS	
Other	

Further details:	
Is the software title part of a toolkit or is it sold on its own?	
Foundation Learning Area or KS1/2Curriculum subject (list more than 1 if necessary):	
Is there a stated age range? If so, what is it?	
Does the onscreen reading age appear to match the stated age range?	
What learning style does this software title seek to support? Is the child going to be active or passive throughout using this title?	
If you could predict its usefulness what would you say – Would it be useful as a learning resource?	
If it were to be chosen as a content rich resource, would it make the material accessible and usable by the children or by you as a teacher?	
If it were to be used as a tool, would it allow the child to think creatively and independently at the same time as developing their subject knowledge?	

Ease of use and navigability:	
Were the children able to use the software successfully and independently (after initial input)? Provide details to back your assertions.	
Was there any confusion about how to navigate through the screens? Again, please provide details to back up your assertions.	
Was any confusion generated by explanations made in the software or were these explanations clear and unambiguous? How was this overcome?	

Recommendations:	
Would you recommend this piece of software to your colleagues, your tutor or class teacher–mentor? What adaptations, if any, would you recommend them to make in order to enhance its use?	

Evaluation and follow-up

Did the framework enable you to make a first judgement about the software? How much background knowledge of the children was important? How much technical knowledge did you need to answer any of the questions? Would you use the framework as it is or would you make some adaptations to it? If so, what would you add or take away? (Remember, we will be considering the child's view in a later activity.)

The TEEM website and associated guidance at www.teem.org.uk

If you feel you have successfully completed the task, return to the needs analysis table and mark it off with the date. Ask your mentor or tutor about being able to use this activity as evidence of meeting the Standards for QTS.

Chapter 3 Making the connections between subject schemes and plans

Link to Professional Standards for QTS

Paragraph 3.3.10

'Those awarded Qualified Teacher Status must demonstrate (that) they use ICT effectively in their teaching.'

Essential background

This theme is concerned with looking at the ways in which ICT resources can be placed within a subject area context. The activity provides a first step in the process. It requires that you are familiar with some of the software categories used in the theme of Evaluating ICT resources (content-rich, tool, courseware, assessment, etc. If you are not, see the previous activity on **pages 62–64**).

Each of these software types may have a direct application in a subject in the primary curriculum. When you compile the list in the activity below, you may find that all subjects are possible with some tools and with others, only some. Likewise, you may find some courseware restrictive but other titles allow you to work in a cross-curricular way.

In terms of the Foundation Stage there are specific Early Years titles which lend themselves to specific learning areas, and specific uses of those titles (refer to the theme on progression, continuity and issues of assessment in ICT for further details, in particular to the activity on **pages 32–36**).

When you carry out the activity below it is worth asking the ICT co-ordinator whether she or he made all of the purchases of the software or whether some resources came out of individual subject areas concerned. This will give you some indication of the overall organisation of ICT in the school and you can relate it to your findings in the activity on **pages 45–48**.

A further issue that you should consider relates to organisation by year group. Which year groups have access to which software titles? Are there some that have a place only in Key Stage 2?

If the titles have been installed on a network, are the titles accessible to all users of the network? Did the titles come with the network or classroom computers or have they been purchased since? If they have been purchased by someone at the school, if you come to use them, you may have a port of call for troubleshooting.

Finally, listing software titles by application in subject areas builds awareness of software titles themselves and gives you a reference chart for planning for curriculum uses. It is the software equivalent of grouping web addresses into folders in Bookmarks or Favourites, as considered earlier (see **pages 55–59**).

The activity should really be carried out in the school environment with co-operation from the school based tutor, class teacher–mentor or ICT co-ordinator as applicable in your situation.

Task

Compile a table in Word (using skills developed previously outside of this self-study guide or in the activities on **pages 77–80**) which includes the following elements:

SOFTWARE TYPE: Tool, Content Rich, Courseware, Assessment, ILS, Other (see above for explanations)
SUBJECTS/LEARNING AREAS:

⮑ English (incl. Literacy)
⮑ Maths (incl. Numeracy)
⮑ Science
⮑ ICT
⮑ Art
⮑ Music
⮑ Geography
⮑ History
⮑ RE
⮑ PE
⮑ PSHE
⮑ Citizenship

Try to list according to age phase supported, or produce two tables, one for each Key Stage.

For the Foundation Stage Curriculum, list under the following headings:

⮑ Personal, social and emotional development
⮑ Language and literacy
⮑ Mathematical development
⮑ Knowledge and understanding of the world
⮑ Physical development
⮑ Creative development

Evaluation/follow-up

Was it easy to group the software by subject category?

Was there already a list that you could adapt?

If you need a piece of software in a given subject, is it easy for you locate it on the computer in your classroom or on the network?

Meeting the Standards

If you feel you have successfully completed the task, return to the needs analysis table and mark it off with the date. Ask your mentor or tutor about being able to use this activity as evidence of meeting the Standards for QTS.

Chapter 3   Progression, continuity and issues of assessment in ICT

Link to Professional Standards for QTS

Paragraph 2.1b

'Those awarded Qualified Teacher Status must demonstrate (that) they have a secure knowledge and understanding of the subjects they are trained to teach … to be able to teach them in the age range for which they are trained, (and that they) have sufficient understanding of a range of work (in NC subjects including) ICT…'

Essential background

For teachers at Key Stage 1 & 2
The background assumed for this activity, which looks at planning for developing ICT skills, is a working knowledge of the QCA scheme of work, or similar, for ICT. There is a discussion of this in some detail in Chapter 2 (**pages 32–36**).

For teachers in the Foundation Stage
The background knowledge assumed for teachers in Early Years settings is a working knowledge of the curriculum for the Foundation Stage. There is a discussion of how this relates to the use of ICT by young children in Chapter 2 (**pages 32–36**). It is best to go straight to the second part of the activity described below.

This activity should be carried out at home and in school.

Task 1: for teachers and KS1 and KS2
Identify a unit of work in the QCA scheme which refers to the age group you are teaching. Find an activity from within the unit which fits in with the current units of work being undertaken in any of the other subject curriculum areas. Plan an activity using the scheme of work to guide you under the following headings:

- ⮑ Lesson overview
- ⮑ School/class context
- ⮑ Learning needs of the children
- ⮑ Grouping/timing
- ⮑ Resources
- ⮑ Theoretical context
- ⮑ N.C./Foundation Stage context
- ⮑ Scheme of work context
- ⮑ Your own learning needs
- ⮑ Organisational memory joggers
- ⮑ Other adults
- ⮑ Learning objectives
- ⮑ Differentiation
- ⮑ Learning needs – EAL
- ⮑ Learning needs – SEN
- ⮑ Assessment opportunities
- ⮑ Key questions
- ⮑ Lesson format
- ⮑ Evaluating the lesson part 1 – operational issues
- ⮑ Evaluating the lesson part 2 – learning outcomes
- ⮑ Evaluating the lesson part 3 – next time

If your school does not use the QCA scheme, then use the school scheme but make additional notes which cross-reference to the government documents. Familiarity with the QCA document will help if you find yourself in a school which uses it for all ICT planning.

Evaluation and follow-up

How easy was the QCA document to work with?

Were you able to plan from it successfully?

Did you find that you had the resources to work with in the school?

Which aspects of the lesson required adaptations to the plan?

Are you now more familiar with both the structure of the QCA scheme of work for ICT and with the National Curriculum requirements for ICT as a subject in its own right?

Task 2: for teachers in the Foundation Stage:

For those in an Early Years placement or Early Years specialist trainees, choose one of the areas of learning, and identify, with the help of the Early Years team at the school, an appropriate piece of software with which the children are already familiar.

Set the computer up within some kind of role play context if possible (if space allows and if it fits with the current planning in the setting). Observe the children working with the software over a period of a few days for a few minutes each day. Ask for one or other of the co-workers in the setting to do the same. Collate your observations.

Evaluation and follow-up

Did the Curriculum Guidance for the Foundation Stage make it easy to plan for ICT?

Did you need to use any additional books or tutor or adult support?

How has the presence of the computer assisted in generating talk around the area of learning?

Have you been able to observe any interactions in which peer learning was evident?

Did the children work in the ways which you expected?

Were there any surprising outcomes?

Were there any overlapping areas of development from the other early learning goals?

The Scheme of Work for ICT
The Curriculum Guidance for the Foundation Stage

If you feel you have successfully completed the task, return to the needs analysis table and mark it off with the date. Ask your mentor or tutor about being able to use this activity as evidence of meeting the Standards for QTS.

Chapter 3   Developing children's ICT skills

Link to Professional Standards for QTS

Paragraph 2.1b

'Those awarded Qualified Teacher Status must demonstrate (that) they have a secure knowledge and understanding of the subjects they are trained to teach … to be able to teach them in the age range for which they are trained, (and that they) have sufficient understanding of a range of work (in NC subjects including) ICT…'

Essential background

This activity assumes that you are aware of the issues around managing ICT resources in your setting, whether it is in an ICT suite or working with the computer(s) in the classroom. There is a discussion of these issues earlier in the chapter (**pages 49–52**).

This activity can be carried out at home and at school.

Make the activity appropriate to your needs and to your location. Choose Task 1, 2 or 3.

Task 1
If you are working with one computer in a classroom at this stage, produce a series of resources which allow for ease of management of the ICT resource. Following some of the arguments above, try producing a:

- ⊃ poster with tips for computer use;
- ⊃ poster with some information on it about the parts of the computer;
- ⊃ sheet with a suggested rota on it (check with the class teacher–mentor or tutor first);
- ⊃ display with digital images of the children working at the computer with positive comments about its use, either as captions or in speech bubbles;
- ⊃ poster with reminders about saving, printing and so on.

Task 2
If you are working in an ICT suite or with laptops on a wireless network or in any other networked environment, carry out the same general activity. If you find that there are already examples in the environment of such tips and displays, involve the children in making new ones or producing a guide for parents (or for trainee teachers.) Be age appropriate. Scale the level of your input and involvement to suit the ages and abilities of the children.

Task 3
In an Early Years setting involve the children in making a display or big book around the use of the computer. If this is inappropriate to the stage of development of the children or to the particular setting, create your own guide which you can share with the children or other adults in the setting to enhance the management of the ICT resource.

Evaluation/follow-up
Has the overall management of the ICT become easier as a result of making the issues more public and going over them again? In what ways?

Has the experience been less successful? Why?

What do you think the children gained from being involved and what have you gained by working with them on the issues?

Meadows, J and Leask, M (eds) (2000) *Learning to Teach with ICT in the Primary School*. London: Routledge.

Sharp, J, Potter, J, Allen, A and Loveless, A (2002) *Primary ICT: Knowledge, Understanding & Practice*. Exeter: Learning Matters.

Smith, Helen (1999) *Opportunities for ICT in the Primary School*. Stoke-on-Trent: Trentham Books.

If you feel you have successfully completed the task, return to the needs analysis table and mark it off with the date. Ask your mentor or tutor about being able to use this activity as evidence of meeting the Standards for QTS.

C3 Children's skills

Chapter 3 Developing children's ability to make connections and solve problems

Link to Professional Standards for QTS

Paragraph 2.1b

'Those awarded Qualified Teacher Status must demonstrate (that) they have a secure knowledge and understanding of the subjects they are trained to teach ... to be able to teach them in the age range for which they are trained, (and that they) have sufficient understanding of a range of work (in NC subjects including) ICT...'

Essential background

This activity assumes that you have read and understood the issues described in Chapter 2 on this theme (see **pages 40–41**).

The main purpose of the whole activity is to enable children to see ICT as a subject:

➲ with connections to hundreds of purposes in the 'real' world;
➲ in which information is used, stored, re-cycled, moved and manipulated;
➲ in which you need to be organised and keep track of the files you have made;
➲ in which you need to be prepared to think flexibly and creatively in order to solve problems.

This activity can only be carried out with children in school.

Task 1
For the first part of the activity, ask children to brainstorm the number and range of places that they know ICT exists in the outside world. This can include the devices themselves and the locations or occupations of the various other uses of computers and related technologies.

In a school where concept mapping is more widely used you could ask the children to draw everything they know about computers and their uses in the form of a mental map. This technique is used widely in other curriculum areas, particularly science. Most recently it has been used as part of the IMPACT2 project (see the BECTA research website: www.becta.org.uk/research or the IMPACT2 research pages via www.nottingham.ac.uk)

Task 2
For the second part of the activity take the discussion further with some focused questioning on aspects of computer use in the world of school or outside school to solve particular issues.

➲ How do we track attendance?
➲ How does the library know which books you have borrowed?
➲ When you visit the doctor's surgery how does s/he know so much about you already?
➲ Why do you sometimes get post addressed to people who don't live in your house?

These sorts of questions need to be age appropriate. They don't need a specific curriculum context and can be quite wide ranging. We are working in the area of ICT as a subject in its own right and we are demonstrating how it can touch many areas of life.

Task 3
Since the second part of the activity has been focused mainly on the information handling side of computer use, the third part looks at the creative side of the use of ICT. To an extent it depends on children's experience of technology such as digital video cameras and music recording technology. If they only have limited experience of these at school you could work with more traditional media in this part of the discussion.

Ask children to reflect on how the music they enjoy is put together. Do they think that computers are involved in any way? How? Try to assess the level of their understanding of what is involved. If they have seen this kind of activity going on in school they will have an advantage.

If it is more appropriate, ask them about how their favourite videos or films are put together. Do they think that computers are involved in any way? How? Again, try to assess the level of their understanding of what is involved.

Finally if their experience of new media is limited and there is no access to technology of this kind within easy reach, talk to them about how their favourite magazines or comics are put together. Discuss the desktop publishing involved. Ask them specifically about the sorts of files which go to make up such a publication. Depending on the age of the children involved, this activity leads directly into making such publications as outlined in the activities on **pages 106–108**.

Evaluation/follow-up
Is it possible to gain a picture of what the children need to know about ICT as a result of this activity? Do they see it as a tool with which they can combine different media? Do they see it as a means of making connections between files and subjects? If not, why not? How can they be introduced to activities which allow them to solve problems in a range of contexts?

Meadows, J and Leask, M (eds) (2000) *Learning to Teach with ICT in the Primary School*. London: Routledge.
Passey, Don *et al*. (1997) *Improve your use of IT in Teaching*. Dunstable: Folens.
Sharp, J, Potter, J, Allen, A and Loveless, A (2002) *Primary ICT: Knowledge, Understanding & Practice*. Exeter: Learning Matters.
Smith, Helen (1999) *Opportunities for ICT in the Primary School*. Stoke-on-Trent: Trentham Books.
Somekh, Bridget and Davis, Niki (eds) (1997) *Using Information Technology Effectively in Teaching and Learning*. London: Routledge.

If you feel you have successfully completed the task, return to the needs analysis table and mark it off with the date. Ask your mentor or tutor about being able to use this activity as evidence of meeting the Standards for QTS.

For the activities you have completed in this chapter, you can use the following table to summarise your professional development. Put a line through the activities which you did not need to complete. Where you carried out an activity, rate your confidence level roughly from low to high and make any comments you feel will be useful to you.

THEMES	Getting started activites completed	Confidence level Low → high				Comments
ICT in planning and assessment	**Word Processing** and basic file management					
	Date					
ICT in locating and using resources, including for SEN and EAL	Observing the setting for ICT in a school.					
	Date					
Routine maintenance and connecting external equipment	Learning about the computer					
	Date					
Using the Internet (becoming part of an online community for education)	Learning about the contribution of the Internet to education: sending and receiving **email**, using a **web browser**					
	Date					
Using ICT in curriculum subjects and in the learning areas of the Foundation Stage	Observing children and adults using the computer in subjects and learning areas across a range of software types					
	Date					
Evaluating ICT resources (software, hardware, websites)	Reviewing educational software					
	Date					
Making the connections between subject schemes and plans	Listing available software and making links with subject areas/Thinking about ICT in the Foundation Stage					
	Date					
Progression, continuity and issues of assessment in ICT	Introducing the scheme of work for ICT/ICT in the Foundation Stage					
	Date					
Developing children's ICT concepts and skills	Managing ICT in a range of settings					
	Date					
Developing children's ability to make connections and solve problems	Discussing real and work related examples of ICT with children					
	Date					

You have begun to develop specific aspects of your professional knowledge, understanding and skills across all the themes covered. By the end of this chapter, the combination of your reading and the classroom-based activities will have provided you with a good foundation upon which to build. It is essential that you check that you have evidence to support all the statements within the needs analysis table at this level and you have also cross-referenced this to the Standards required for QTS. It is important to talk to your teacher about your progress at this stage. They will also be able to help you check that you do have appropriate evidence to audit your progress against the Standards. However, you will also need to ensure that you have started to complete the profiling required by your training provider since this may cover additional Standards.

Chapter 4   Developing your Skills ⇒
Introduction

Contents

The activities in this section are aimed at people who are gaining confidence in learning how to use ICT in their personal and professional development, in subject teaching and as a subject in its own right.

The activities described in this section can be carried out in a range of settings. You may have access to your own computer or to a computer in a college or a library in which you can carry out activities relating to personal and professional development. As before, for this strand of development, most activities can be carried out at your own pace, in your own time.

The activities described in the strands of ICT in subject teaching and ICT as a subject in its own right should be carried out in school with access to appropriate hardware and software and, on occasion, to appropriate Internet connections. There will, inevitably, be exceptions to this and not all of the activities in the sections on ICT in subject teaching and ICT as a subject in its own right can be carried out in school. There are occasions when it may be possible or even desirable to do these activities at home or college. In order to help you make a judgement about where each activity may or may not be most suitably carried out, each activity description contains a series of hints which suggest where it could be carried out.

For the purposes of auditing your development during your training, each strand of development is linked to a Professional Standard for QTS. As you complete each piece of evidence you can ask a mentor or visiting tutor to sign to say that this has been achieved. In this way, it can be added to your profiling. Each training provider will approach this in different ways and it is important to link completion of the tasks in this book to the profiling requirements of your training.

The activities in this chapter are arranged as follows:

Themes	Page reference	Activity title	Area of development
ICT in planning and in assessment	Page 77	Using more advanced features in word processing	PERSONAL AND PROFESSIONAL USE OF ICT (cf. QTS standards 2002, para 2.5)
ICT in locating and using resources, including for SEN and EAL	Page 81	Finding out more about school provision/interviewing the ICT co-ordinator	
Routine maintenance and connecting external equipment	Page 83	Learning about the computer continued - basic troubleshooting and maintenance	
Using the Internet (Becoming part of an online community for education)	Page 85	Organising a web browser, searching and finding useful and usable resources for education.	
Using ICT in curriculum subjects and in the learning areas of the Foundation Stage	Page 89	Subject related examples: Using **databases** and **spreadsheets** in maths and science	ICT IN SUBJECT TEACHING (cf. QTS standards 2002, para. 3.3.10)
Evaluating ICT resources (software, hardware, websites)	Page 94	Evaluating the use of a specific learning tool (curriculum example – floor robot)	
Making the connections between subject schemes and plans	Page 96	Planning work in the schemes and strategies: literacy and numeracy	
Progression, continuity and issues of assessment in ICT	Page 99	Beginning to assess children's skills in ICT	ICT AS A SUBJECT IN ITS OWN RIGHT (cf. QTS standards 2002, para. 2.1 b)
Developing children's ICT concepts and skills	Page 103	Involving children in the choice and use of a range of ICT tools	
Developing children's ability to make connections and solve problems	Page 106	Integrating tasks and integrating skills with **presentation** software and desktop publishing	

Each activity is outlined in full and has the following information provided with it:

⮥ a link with the ICT National Curriculum and/or the QCA Scheme of work for ICT (if applicable);
⮥ a link to another subject in the National Curriculum or to its related strategies (for this example, where relevant);
⮥ a QTS skills test link (if applicable);
⮥ a note of the possible Audit point against the QTS standards;
⮥ essential background to the activity including such items as which equipment to use and which setting might be most appropriate for carrying it out;
⮥ a description of the activity and all the elements which go to make it up;
⮥ some ideas on how to evaluate its success;
⮥ finally, some suggested further background reading.

Link to Professional Standards for QTS

Paragraph 2.5

'Those awarded Qualified Teacher Status must demonstrate (that) they know how to use ICT effectively, both to teach their subject and to support their wider professional role' (DFES/TTA, 2002).

Essential background

This activity assumes that you are comfortable with two important sets of skills:

1 Knowing how to navigate your computer, organise files and create any folders which you need to help you to organise your work.
2 Knowing how to open a word processor file, enter some text and save it in a specific place.

These skills will have been practised in the activities for this theme in Chapter 3, but the activities here require you to go a little further with what word processors have to offer you as a teacher. Specifically, they will address the following areas:

1 Importing images into your work
2 Using tables to design formats for planning and assessment
3 Copying and pasting text from one file into another
4 Working with templates

Importing images into your work

You may be surprised to learn that children as young as 7 or 8 are required to know how to import images into their work. In fact, by using bespoke software for children, younger children can be shown how to do it. The means by which you import these images will differ from computer to computer and from software to software. However, they all have the same guiding principle behind them: knowing where your files are stored and being able to find them when you need them. In this case, if you have a place on your computer where you keep regularly used images, a folder called 'My Pictures' for example, you won't find this difficult at all. Some images you use will be there and others, created for sale on CDs of 'clip art' will be found on a CD. Others you will locate on the Internet, and elsewhere in this Strand of Development we will discuss how you can save them into your own folder (see **pages 85–88**).

Open a word processor, for example the most commonly used package on the PC – Microsoft Word. Along the top line you will see the familiar list of menu headings beginning File, Edit, View etc. Find Insert. Click on it and a menu will drop down. (See Fig. 4.1 overleaf.)

You will see a whole range of images that can be inserted. If you choose Clip Art a further menu will take you through a range of images in many different categories which come with the software. If you choose From File, you have the flexibility of navigating anywhere on your computer where images might be and finding your image of choice. Of course, previously, you would have saved any images you needed in a folder helpfully labelled 'My Pictures' and you would know the location of this folder on your computer.

Once you click on Insert, the picture will be embedded in your document. If you click in the middle of it, resizing controls appear at the corners and in the middle of the side. You click and drag on these to adjust the size.

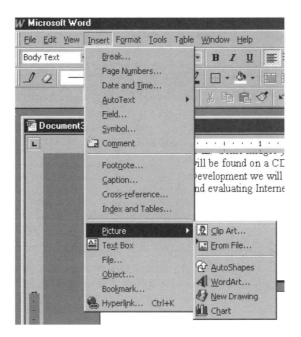

Fig. 4.1 Inserting a picture in Word.

With any modern word processor, the facility to import images is a common tool. If you are not using Word, or if you are not using a PC, you need to look for appropriate, likely looking commands and procedures. You need to consult manuals or ask for support. The feature is certainly there and it will not hurt to try to discover its exact location for yourself.

Remember, although the exact mechanics of inserting images may vary and can usually be discovered by trial and error (or, more rarely, the manual), the importance of being organised and knowing the location of the images you want to use cannot be overstressed. This part of the process is down to you.

Using tables
If you are using Word on either the PC or the Mac, tables have their own little sub-menu, further along the line from Insert. Don't click on Insert at this point or confusion will ensue, since Word also has a facility for creating tables of a different sort here – tables of contents, etc.

Click on Table and specify the number of rows and columns you want. In Word you can also create a table quickly by clicking on a table icon and clicking and dragging to determine the numbers of rows and columns and, eventually, the size of the table.

Copying and pasting from one file to another
A skill which makes full use of the word processor's capacity to reduce workload is that of cutting, copying and pasting. This is a skill which you will also be required to pass on to children at some point. You need to know this. You also need to be able to do this for the QTS skills tests.

In any file on any computer, if you highlight text by clicking and dragging the mouse over it, or by holding down Shift and using the cursor keys, you have marked an area out for cutting, copying and pasting. How you complete the operation depends on your personal preference for using menu commands or keyboard shortcuts.

Using the menu commands prepares you better for the skills tests where the keyboard shortcuts don't work. In this case, highlight the bit you want to copy, click on Edit, then choose Copy. (If you wish to remove this text permanently from the document and put it in another one, choose Cut at this point.) At this stage it may well appear that nothing has really happened. The text is there. It's just stored temporarily in the computer, behind the scenes. Move to the file you want to place the copied text into. Place your mouse at the point where you want the text to appear. Click on Edit and then Paste. The text will appear.

If you want to use a potentially more efficient method, learn the following keyboard shortcuts. After you have chosen your text:

➲ To cut – hold down the Control key and press X at the same time.
➲ To copy – hold down the Control key and press C at the same time.

When you have travelled to where you want to place your cut or copied text:

➲ To paste – hold down the Control key and press V at the same time

You will notice that these three keys are next to each other and adjacent to the Control key. You will find that this works in almost any situation on any computer with a keyboard.

Circumstances in which you may want to learn how to copy and paste:

➲ Using National Curriculum strategy documents for planning. If you have an electronic copy of this, selecting and pasting learning objectives into your planning will save you (literally) hours. This is not cheating. It is using the technology to support you.
➲ Building up a series of useful quotations from relevant theory in a folder labelled 'Theory' or similar. Using these for copying and pasting into planning. Again, this is not cheating. It is using the technology to support you.

There are many other circumstances in which you might use cutting, copying and pasting and you can make decisions about when and how to use it most effectively.

Templates
Most word processors offer you the option to make a file, save it as a document template and use a blank copy of it over and over again thereafter. In Word you can find this in the Save As dialogue after clicking on File.

Circumstances under which you may want to use templates:

➲ creating files you use again and again, e.g planning pro formas, weekly forecasts, timesheets, ticksheets, rotas, etc.
➲ creating on screen activities for children in word processors (see the discussion on **pages 28–31**).

This activity can be carried out on any computer to which you have access at home, school, college, library, etc.

Task1: working with images in your word processor
Open a file and type a brief letter home about activities which will be going on in school across a half term in three or four different areas. A few lines of text will do. Make the language appropriate to parents. At the top of the letter or at the bottom, insert images which relate to each of the areas. Use the available clip art. Where no clip art is available, you will have to cross reference with the activity on **pages 85–88** and go onto the Internet and get some. Make notes to help you remember how to do it.

Task 2: working with tables in your word processor
Open a file and discover how to make your page into a landscape format. In Word this option is in File, Page Setup, under Paper Size (bizarrely, since the size doesn't change). Create a table with enough rows and columns for you to put in the days of the week, and the sessions of each day. You now have a weekly timetable/planner. Make notes to help you remember how to do it.

Task 3: working with cutting and pasting
Open up the document that you created in Task 1. Locate one of the sentences in which you describe work in a curriculum area this half term. Select it and copy it. Start up a new file and paste the text into it. Save it under a new filename. Make notes to help you remember how to do it.

Task 4: working with templates
Open the file you made in Task 2. Add the title 'My teaching sessions: Week beginning …'

Leave a space for the date. Save the file as a template using the Save As command in the File menu. Give it a title, such as 'Sessions template'. Close the file. Now click on the word New in the File menu. A list of choices of file templates to use should pop up. One of them will be 'Sessions template'. You can now use this blank weekly forecast to type in the sessions during the week where you will be taking the class (and indicate the areas where you won't during this particular week). You can save this as a file, labelled 'Sessions week beginning (and insert the correct date here)'. Being an organised user of the computer, you will have made a folder previously labelled 'Weekly sessions forecast' in which to place these files. Make notes to help you remember how to do it.

Evaluation/follow-up

Note down for each of the tasks, where the difficulties were, if there were any. Make a development plan to address them. It may be that you need to ask for help from a tutor or colleague. Perhaps you need to read one of the many manuals and alternative guides to the major pieces of software available. Some of the elements above may take time to become part of your use of the computer of you are unfamiliar with them. All of them will save you time, make you more efficient, make your work more attractive and help you to get to know about the speed and automatic functions of ICT more quickly.

Guides to the uses of Word by publishers such as *QUE* books or the *Dummies Guides* to using your word processor or particular computer.

Terry Freedman's book on *Managing with ICT* (2000) contains many tips for using ICT to help you with your role.

If you feel you have successfully completed the task, return to the needs analysis table and mark it off with the date. Ask your mentor or tutor about being able to use this activity as evidence of meeting the Standards for QTS.

Chapter 4   ICT in locating and using resources

Link to Professional Standards for QTS

Paragraph 2.5

'Those awarded Qualified Teacher Status must demonstrate (that) they know how to use ICT effectively, both to teach their subject and to support their wider professional role.'

Essential background

This activity presumes that you are familiar with the general provision of ICT resources in the school, following the questions which you raised in the activity on **pages 49–52** (or had discovered already, independently).

The activity assumes that you are able to make contact with the school ICT co-ordinator. This assumes that there is one. In some schools the ICT co-ordinator role will be non-existent or an unfilled vacancy. Where an ICT co-ordinator is appointed, there will be wide variations in her/his status in the school. Sometimes, ICT co-ordinators are members of the senior management team with responsibility for making bids for government funding and training. In other situations there is nominally an ICT co-ordinator but they have very little budgetary responsibility and are expected to act at a very basic level (for example, replacing the cartridges in printers). We have already discussed why there are such wide variations in levels of provision overall. The existence and relative status of an ICT co-ordinator are other indicating factors.

If you are able to identify an ICT co-ordinator, they can probably assist you in a number of ways. For example, by:

➲ giving you access to the school network;
➲ providing you with a school ICT policy;
➲ giving you some insight into the school development plan and local/national priorities;
➲ going through the school scheme of work with you and talking to you about progression;
➲ giving you some idea of the context of the school in terms of the overall ICT achievements of the children;
➲ talking to you about INSET which the staff have undertaken recently, including training under the New Opportunities Fund scheme.

Where there is no ICT co-ordinator, the activity should consist of a deeper level of investigation of the resources and their layout than in the activity in Chapter 3 for this theme. There is also an expectation that you will attempt to find out, tactfully, about levels of skill and training amongst the staff. This will also enable you to know who to approach for finding out

This activity must be carried out at school.

Preparation

This activity focuses on the people who impact on the organisation and use of ICT in the school. Find out who they are in your particular school situation.

Task

Interview them and discover more about their influence on the whole school development for ICT.

For example, you could ask them, sensitively, if they are:

➲ unpaid co-ordinators; or
➲ given one responsibility point; or
➲ given two responsibility points.

Try to find out whether they are working solely on developing ICT or combining ICT with one or more of Science, Maths, Technology or, less usually, English or a creative arts subject.

For ICT co-ordinators or senior managers in charge of ICT, try to discover the following information about them.

➲ their training;
➲ how they got the job;
➲ what contact they have with their LEA advisory team;
➲ their role in the management structure of the school;
➲ their budget;
➲ how they pass on their expertise;
➲ what sort of role they take in troubleshooting (do they take on minor repairs themselves, or do they encourage others to learn more about the ICT in their school?);
➲ do they report faults or have a system for doing so?
➲ is there a service contract?
➲ crucially, is there a development plan for ICT and how was it constructed?
➲ how do they involve parents and carers, classroom assistants, governors and others in ICT in the school?
➲ have they been or are they about to become involved in a whole-staff training programme for ICT (such as the one funded by the NOF)?
➲ what was the outcome of the most recent inspection in terms of ICT and how is the school addressing the issues?

Relate the findings to the development of ICT in other subjects. Are there policy statements or schemes of work which outline how ICT can be developed in other subjects? Is there evidence to suggest that it is happening in the school?

Evaluation/follow-up

Do you have a greater understanding of the situation in terms of ICT at the school? Could you outline what facilities are available to someone who asked you about the school? Do you know where to go for support and advice in your time at this school? Do you know where the scheme of work for ICT is and could you use it in your planning? If you can answer these questions, you have completed the activity successfully.

For information on the training of teachers to use ICT in their subject teaching, visit the NOF website at www.nof.gov.uk/ict

For information on whole school development see the BECTA website www.becta.org.uk

If you feel you have successfully completed the activity, return to the needs analysis table and mark it off with the date. Ask your mentor or tutor about being able to use this activity as evidence of meeting the Standards for QTS.

Chapter 4   Routine maintenance and connecting equipment

Link to Professional Standards for QTS

Paragraph 2.5

'Those awarded Qualified Teacher Status must demonstrate (that) they know how to use ICT effectively, both to teach their subject and to support their wider professional role.'

Essential background

As you read in Chapter 2, teachers are not expected to perform major technical work. The following question is often raised, 'Where do the boundaries lie in terms of what you are expected to be able to do?'

As a minimum as a class teacher the following items might be good starting points:

- knowing how to switch the computer on;
- knowing how to log on to the network (if applicable, of which more later);
- knowing how to connect to the Internet (if applicable, as above);
- knowing how to run a selection of software for children and for her or himself;
- knowing how to print;
- knowing how to print on more than one printer (if applicable);
- knowing how to put a disk or CD into the drive and access it;
- knowing the importance of saving and retrieving work;
- knowing how to connect commonly used equipment;
- knowing how to label files and how to look for them if they are lost;
- knowing what to check in the event of any of the following:
  - the screen freezing;
  - no sound from the speakers;
  - no image on the monitor;
  - printing not happening;
  - a web page not loading;
- finally, knowing how to log off and knowing how to switch off.

There is a further series of tasks which you may need to be able to carry out with regard to regular maintenance. These include such things as changing ink cartridges and so on. Whether or not you or a technician or the ICT co-ordinator will do this is something that needs to be negotiated. If in doubt, always ask about the boundaries of expectation in terms of technical support.

Networks

Many primary schools spent their allocation of NGfL money on networks of various sorts. This undoubtedly has an impact on organisation and on your level of interaction with individual computers. It is less likely that you would need to know about connections at the back of the machine in such a setting. Nevertheless it would be worth asking your ICT co-ordinator about the peripheral devices being used with the network and how they connect.

The network room as a setting impacts on pedagogy and there will be a full discussion of both positive and negative aspects of this in the sections on ICT in subject teaching and ICT as a subject in its own right. Network rooms are sometimes isolated from the rest of the school, a series of 10–15 computers connected together with no connection back into the classrooms. In other schools, there are connections between a discrete network room and classroom computers or even portable computers. We will discuss the pedagogical issues arising from this when we look at organisation for teaching and learning in other activities.

In terms of technical knowledge, it is most important that you and your children know how to log on. When you are placed in the school on a teaching practice, ask about having a guest log in name so that you can explore the network software and how it operates. The children you teach will also need to be made network aware.

Hardware problems and software problems

Although it is not always immediately obvious, some problems you have to deal with are to do with the physical machinery, the hardware. Some problems are to do with the software, which is what you see on screen, what the computer runs and you try to use. The two are of course interconnected. When fault-finding, however, you need to be aware of both and check them.

For example, imagine a situation where the children are using a piece of software which runs maths games. They can't hear the instructions or the music accompanying the game. You have to sort it out.

First, remembering that the hardware may be responsible (the actual physical machinery of the computer and the speakers themselves), check that the sound is turned up or down on the speakers. Check the volume control. Before even doing that, check that the speakers are actually switched on and receiving power. If they are, check that the physical connections between the computer and the speaker haven't been broken. Sometimes, just because they can, children pull out the cables from behind computers.

If the cables are intact and the speakers are receiving power, you need to check for problems in the software. Perhaps the sound has been switched off on screen. On a windows PC, look for a loudspeaker icon on the taskbar at the bottom of the screen. Double click on it to bring up a control panel for sound. Make sure that the box underneath the main volume control labelled 'Mute' is not ticked. If it is, untick it. If this doesn't work, look for volume controls in the maths software itself. You will find this in a page labelled 'Teacher Options' or similar.

If all this fails, call for support from someone else, e.g. the ICT co-ordinator, technician, classroom assistant, or a child. Admitting you sometimes don't know how to do something makes you human. Computers are frustrating at times and half of the frustration can be alleviated by accepting that things can and will go wrong and by sharing and looking for solutions with other people.

The following activity can be carried out anywhere.

Task
Create a flow chart to identify the causes and solutions to one or more of the following:

- ⮕ the sound does not appear to be working (based on the process above);
- ⮕ there is no 'picture' on the monitor;
- ⮕ there is no printout from the printer.

Evaluation/follow-up
Some or all of the above will involve very detailed descriptions of what is involved. The printer, in particular can be a complex issue (although it often boils down to being offline, having no paper, the ink having run out or a program crash). Provided you have outlined the reasons for your choices and diagnostic path through them, this activity will have been completed successfully. Some older children might enjoy this particular activity and will have many suggestions as to how to fix the computer or printer.

Meeting the standards

If you feel you have successfully completed the task, return to the needs analysis table and mark it off with the date. Ask your mentor or tutor about being able to use this activity as evidence of meeting the standards for QTS.

Chapter 4 — Becoming part of an online community for education

Link to Professional Standards for QTS

Paragraph 2.5

'Those awarded Qualified Teacher Status must demonstrate (that) they know how to use ICT effectively, both to teach their subject and to support their wider professional role.'

Essential background

This activity assumes that you are familiar with the basics of using a web browser to view web pages and move between them. In other words, it assumes a level of skill consistent with the relevant parts of the activity on **pages 55–59**:

- ⮥ knowing how to visit a website using a web browser;
- ⮥ knowing how to save the location for another time so that you don't need to remember the address (using 'Favourites' and 'Bookmarks').

The four parts of the activity provide you with the opportunity to practise a useful set of additional skills which make it possible for you to:

- ⮥ use your web browser more effectively;
- ⮥ save resources from the Internet;
- ⮥ search for particular resources;
- ⮥ make a basic judgement about what you find.

Use your web browser more effectively

Firstly, your web browser can become disorganised as you add more and more favourites (if you use Internet Explorer) or bookmarks (if you use Netscape) to it. Ultimately, launching it and attempting to negotiate a long list of websites in no particular order leads to frustration. You can, and should, organise your frequently visited sites into folders. In Internet Explorer, this is achieved by clicking on Organise Favourites and following the instructions on making new folders. In Netscape, the same task is achieved by clicking on Bookmarks, then Edit Bookmarks and then File and New Folder (see Fig. 4.2 overleaf).

You could create folders based on curriculum areas, personal interest and so on. The next time you are browsing the web and you want to save a link as a favourite or bookmark you can choose to place it in the correct folder at the time that you add it.

Save resources from the Internet

When you visit a web page, you may want to save an image or a piece of text, or the whole web page. Having made folders to store things such as 'Useful images' or 'Useful documents', you can proceed to locate and save resources.

Most documents, sounds, images, and video clips on the Internet are in a form that can be easily recognised and read by your computer. Occasionally, if your computer has not been set up correctly, you may not be able to view certain kinds of resources.

Many large documents on government sites, such as those on the OFSTED website and elsewhere, are held in a format known as PDF (Portable Document Format). The idea behind this is that this file format is understood by all computers everywhere, provided that the reader software has been installed. This reader software is called Adobe Acrobat Reader. It doesn't cost anything. It can be downloaded from the Adobe website (follow the link on, for example, the OFSTED site) free of charge.

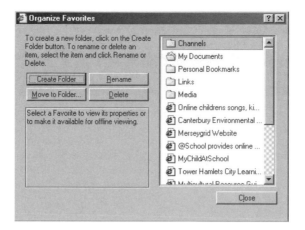

Above: the 'Organize Favorites' dialogue box in Internet Explorer
Below: the 'Bookmarks' organisation area in Netscape

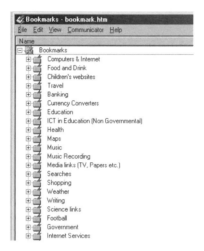

Fig. 4.2 Organising your browser.

Most computers have this software pre-installed and it is launched automatically by your browser. It is probable that you have been using Acrobat Reader without even knowing it's happening.

Some sites store documents as Word files. When you click on the link, the browser attempts to find Word on your computer and starts to load it as the file is being downloaded. On these occasions, and when Acrobat Reader is required, you may want to simply download the file and look at it later. This would be the case if you were connecting and paying the phone bill by the minute because it invariably takes longer. It is recommended that you download files that you need, save them into the right folders and then read them at your leisure.

The method for downloading any file to your local computer is to click on the link to the filename with the RIGHT mouse button and then choose Save Target As (if you are using Internet Explorer) and then, in the window which pops up, direct the file into the folder of your choice on your computer. On an Apple computer, hold down Control and click and do the same thing. For Netscape, replace Save Target As with Save Link As.

If you want to save an image file from the Internet, do exactly the same thing, clicking in the middle of the image with the RIGHT mouse button and then follow the Save Image As dialogue as appropriate.

Searching

You can't always immediately find what you are looking for on the Internet. A number of web pages exist which are there solely to search for you. These are called search engines.

It is worth pointing out that searching the Internet for a particular curriculum resource from scratch can be a laborious activity. It is usually better to visit a site with established and verified links (see below on the TeacherNet pages).

However, if you need a particular focused item, as opposed to a completely created classroom resource and you are determined to search yourself, here are two recommended links (there are many more):

➲ Ask Jeeves: www.ask.co.uk. This search engine allows you to enter a question using natural language into the dialogue box. So you could type 'Where can I find a map of Melbourne in Australia?' The Jeeves search engine would return in a matter of seconds with many links to sites offering maps of Melbourne and Australia and all manner of related items. You would follow the links returned to you and decide which is the best for you.
➲ Google: www.google.com. This search engine actually searches many other search engines and returns thousands of results. It is very popular and very powerful. In this case, you enter words or phrases in the search dialogue box. There are ways of doing this so that you save yourself time and stress. If you are looking for information about the Emperor Penguin and you type Emperor Penguin into the search box, your search results will show all pages with both words in them (many millions of results). If, on the other hand you type Emperor + Penguin, your search engine will return every page it can find with both Emperor and Penguin on it – but not necessarily together. To find the information you are looking for you would need to locate pages where the two words were next to each other and you would need to type the following into the search box: 'Emperor Penguin'.

Searching in this way takes practice and there is help available on the Internet itself. Most search engine sites have 'How to…' pages on them. There is also extensive advice in guides such as *The Rough Guide to the Internet*.

Searching with children

It cannot have escaped your notice that there is a vast amount of unsuitable material on the Internet. Searching with Google or Ask Jeeves will often find it in amongst your innocent searches by accident rather than intent. It makes sense to use these search engines with caution. When searching with children it is best to use search engines which have been created to be safe by means of various filtering devices. Try the following:

➲ Ask Jeeves for kids: www.ajkids.com
➲ Yahooligans: www.yahooligans.com

Resources for teaching

Of most interest and use to you are probably the sites which will provide you with curriculum advice and resources. This was one of the main reasons for the government connecting schools to the Internet in the first place and one of the driving forces behind the NGfL. Recently, the government websites have started to evaluate and organise resources for particular age phases and in particular subjects. You can visit these sites knowing that you will find something of relevance and that it will have been reviewed and evaluated by a teacher. You may find that you do not want to use it when you see it, but these resources are, if nothing else, valuable starting points for you.

Amongst the resources you can find for teaching are:

➲ lesson plans
➲ lesson resources
➲ worksheets (some of variable use and quality, like all 'worksheets')
➲ images (art galleries for example)
➲ museum sites
➲ subject sites
➲ languages sites for EAL and multicultural education
➲ Special Educational Needs sites

The places to find approved sites – as a starting point – are via links on:

➲ Teachernet: www.teachernet.gov.uk
➲ Becta: www.becta.org.uk

Two popular, non-governmental websites include:

➲ Educate the children: www.educate.org.uk
➲ Primary resources: www.primaryresources.co.uk

Three popular media sites with good, onward links and resources are:

➔ BBC learning: www.bbc.co.uk/learning
➔ Channel 4's learning site: www.4learning.co.uk
➔ The Guardian's education pages: www.educationunlimited.co.uk

Remember to be organised with folders ready on your computer for resources in the form of word files, PDF files, image files and so on.

These links are only starting points and examples. There are many, many more and you and your colleagues will find your own favourites and most useful ones. The best websites for education to bookmark or add to your favourites are those which maintain further, onward links. It may be that you college tutor or placement school maintains lists of links and you could start there.

This activity could be carried out at home, college or in your placement school on a computer to which you have regular access.

Task 1

Open up the browser which you use most frequently and make some folders within your favourites (Internet Explorer) or bookmarks (Netscape). Try the following (or make up your own):

➔ maths;
➔ literacy;
➔ maps;
➔ government sites;
➔ music.

Task 2

As an exercise in finding pages, find the QCA, the DfES and the NGfL and put all these pages into your favourites or bookmarks in the correct (government sites) folder. Then find a website for your favourite musical style, musician or performer and save it in your music, bookmarks or favourites folder.

Task 3

As an exercise in finding resources, find a science lesson plan or resource at the appropriate age phase for you or for the Knowledge and Understanding of the World part of the Foundation curriculum. Save this as a file in a folder on your hard disk labelled 'Science resources'.

➔ Find a map of Sierra Leone and save it as an image file on your computer in an appropriate folder.
➔ Find a painting by the artist Mary Cassatt and save this as an image file on your computer.

Evaluation/follow-up

Were you able to organise your bookmarks or favourites into categories?

What difficulties did you have with saving different file types from the Internet (if any)?

Were you able to support colleagues who were experiencing difficulties?

Have you seen any good examples of curriculum materials?

Were you able to navigate around the government sites for education?

For the mechanics of saving and locating web pages, try Kennedy, A (2001) *The Rough Guide to the Internet*. London: Rough Guides.

If you feel you have successfully completed the task, return to the needs analysis table and mark it off with the date. Ask your mentor or tutor about being able to use this activity as evidence of meeting the Standards for QTS.

Chapter 4 — Using ICT in curriculum subjects and in the learning areas of the Foundation Stage

Link to Professional Standards for QTS

Paragraph 3.3.10

'Those awarded Qualified Teacher Status must demonstrate (that) they use ICT effectively in their teaching.'

Essential background

The aim of this activity is to explore the link between the uses of software tools and development in a curriculum subject or learning area. In the activity of **pages 96–99**, you will see how specific ICT tools, which are designed with the young learner's conceptual development in mind at the outset, operate in curriculum subjects. In this activity however, the emphasis is on the use of content free software or tools which can be applied in subjects such as mathematics or science.

Databases are used in school to support curriculum development in many subjects. They allow children to store information, to retrieve it, add to it, represent it in different ways and to ask questions of it.

The ways in which databases are introduced can have an effect on how successful or otherwise teaching and learning with them can be. If you launch the subject of databases with children with data collection, the children are saddled with a laborious task which has no obvious point or ending to it. Beginning with data handling without first interrogating data in a pre-created database is essentially going the wrong way about it. At the same time as you interrogate data, you can be introducing terminology which will be useful to them in all areas. At the very least, children should know the rough definitions of such terms as field, record and file as well as the hierarchical nature of these concepts. Interrogating databases which have been created previously also allows for the possibility of placing deliberately false information into the class domain. Asking children to question the veracity or otherwise of the data in a database is part of the process of understanding the workings of ICT in the wider world.

Having decided to introduce the terminology, the next issue is to locate appropriate tools which allow you to be developmental, even to differentiate in your planning. Black Cat provide curriculum software which is scalable, that is to say it allows for users of different ages and abilities. Titles include Pick a Picture (for Early Years and Key Stage 1) and Information Workshop (for Key Stages 1 and 2). There are other examples and you will come across them in the various toolkits which are supplied to schools in the wake of funding in the era of the NGfL. The software mentioned also comes with example databases set up for you to explore before you begin to create your own with the children.

Mathematics and science are two example subjects which provide curriculum related contexts for the use of databases. Once children are comfortable with the concepts of fields, records and files there are many topics which you can use. Within science for example, subjects such as Ourselves, Materials, Plants and Animals lend themselves to the collection of small, manageable amounts of data which nonetheless allow the speed and automatic functions of ICT to be demonstrated. You could ask the children to suggest field names and use tools which allow these to be altered and develop as the topic develops. Tools which allow for such flexibility should be an integral part of any software toolkit because they allow children to think creatively and to ask questions about both the topic and the tool.

Mathematics requires children to have opportunities to manipulate data. Having used a curriculum context for the collection of such data, the mathematical possibilities of graphing, of different ways of displaying the data come into play. Children should be asked to think critically about the way that they represent data. The databases they use are as powerful in their way as Office tools and can graph results of searches and sorts in many different ways. Children should be asked to justify the choices of graph that they make. Which ones are the most readable? Which ones allow for the most number of questions and further investigations? Which ones prove or disprove particular points?

The ICT binds the topics together and allows children to put together the skills and knowledge which they are acquiring in many subject areas in the same space. In an era in which the primary curriculum has been allowed to become atomised, ICT is uniquely positioned to make some of the connections again, allowing children to explore and learn in ways that most suit their curiosity and exploit their potential as problem solvers.

Spreadsheets in both mathematics and science also allow for the asking of such questions and the modelling of new relationships and further problems. In mathematics, they can be used to explore the relationships between numbers in a series using the Fill tool. They can be used to generate simple scenarios such as the shop suggested below. For science, they can hold information which is changing and perform calculations on it. If you have access to datalogging equipment, you can record data from the environment and put it straight into a spreadsheet from where calculations can be performed.

Children can learn about how information can be represented from the earliest years. In early Key Stage 1, tools such as 2graph in 2Simple Software's Infant Video Toolkit, allow for the creation of simple graphs. Black Cat's Pick a Picture introduces the concept of a record and the fields it contains without making it difficult, in a simple point and click environment. These pieces of software need to be used appropriately and when the children are ready for it, in line with their own developing knowledge in the mathematics curriculum.

In the Foundation Stage, these tools are not appropriate unless grounded in a particular experience and set up in that way. A tally for dinners or simple collection of data related to a walk or other activity is all that is required at this stage and, even then, only if appropriate and if arising from the learning areas being explored.

The following activity requires that you keep these concepts in mind:

⊃ databases and spreadsheets must be introduced in a curriculum context;
⊃ databases and spreadsheets should be used in a scalable way with tools that allow you to differentiate;
⊃ databases and spreadsheets should serve the purpose of the subject and not the other way round;
⊃ databases and spreadsheets have their own terminology which should be used accurately and encouraged;
⊃ in the early years of primary school, children can be shown that computers can represent information in simple graphic form (if it is appropriate to do so – see above).

The activity should take place in school with children

Task 1

This task is to interrogate an example database with children. First, familiarise them with the common terminology used in databases:

⊃ Field – a description of a heading under which information is collected. In a database about Ourselves, field names could include name, age, height, eye colour and others.
⊃ Record – a collection of a set of fields. In a database about Ourselves, the complete set of fields for one person would constitute a record.
⊃ File – a collection of a set of records. In a database about Ourselves, the complete set of records collected for a whole class would constitute a file.

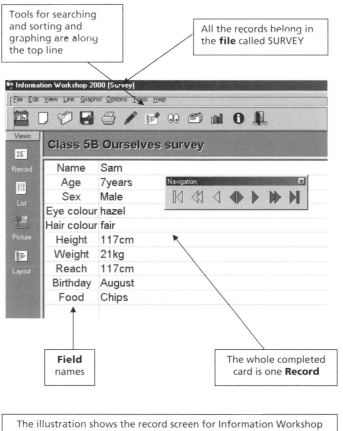

The illustration shows the record screen for Information Workshop 2000, a primary data handling software title.

Fig. 4.3 Screenshot from Black Cat's Information Workshop 2000.

Use some of the tools provided by the software to raise questions about the data. Using the Sort tool, arrange the data according to the values in one of the fields. In a database about Ourselves this could be a sort on age of child, arranged with the youngest first.

In a database about Ourselves, use the graphing tools to display the range of birthdays in a particular month, or the spread of handspan size in the class.

Task 2: Set up a database with the children
Using your Internet connection in advance, view example lessons using databases on the Internet. The Kent Grid for Learning has an example of some work done in a Year 4 class on friction. It describes how to go about setting up the activity, the ICT skills required in advance and the science context as well as how the learning in the subject appeared to progress as the lesson unfolded.

Choose an area of science to investigate that relates to the scheme of work for this time of the year. See the activities linked to making connections between subject schemes and plans in Chapters 3, 4 and 5 for additional ideas on how to draw connections between schemes of work and available software.

For children in the Foundation Stage, a database is going to be inappropriate. Some graphical work could still be used alongside images of the children to make the experience more direct and less abstract. Very young children are using appropriate software such as 2graph (part of the 2simple Infant Video Toolkit). However, if it proves that this is not possible, working with a smaller group of children out of your usual age phase would be one way forward. The experiences which you have working in this way with the children will be useful in relation to your own personal use of ICT including rehearsing for the ICT skills test.

Task 3: Using a simple spreadsheet with children
If you have access to a good primary school spreadsheet you can carry out this task easily. If you are stuck with Microsoft Excel it is still possible but needs adaptation according to the age of the children. RM's Number Magic or Black Cat's Number Box are good examples (both available in toolkits from RM and Granada Learning respectively). If it is not possible to do this activity with children you can still work at home or college on simple spreadsheet concepts.

One activity would be to generate times tables using the Fill facility. If you start to type numbers in a column going down the screen and then click the Fill tool, the primary school spreadsheet will assume that you are working on a series of numbers. In Excel you will need to specify what kind of series you are producing. You will also need to make the cells bigger (upwards of 20 point font) and closer to the appearance of a primary school spreadsheet to make the experience more accessible.

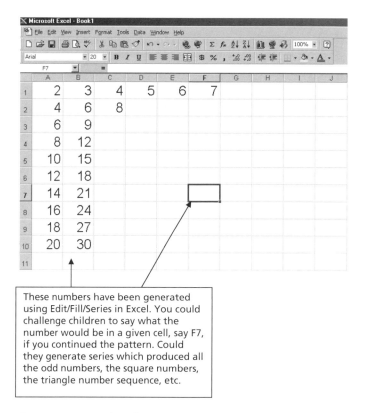

These numbers have been generated using Edit/Fill/Series in Excel. You could challenge children to say what the number would be in a given cell, say F7, if you continued the pattern. Could they generate series which produced all the odd numbers, the square numbers, the triangle number sequence, etc.

Fig. 4.4 Screenshot from Microsoft Excel with adaptations made for children.

You could go further and explore the monitoring of stock in a shop and introduce the power of a spreadsheet to perform functions according to a simple formula. As before, the experiences which you have working in this way with the children will be useful in relation to your own personal use of ICT, including rehearsing for the ICT skills test. In the illustration below, Excel has, once again, been adapted for the purposes of the setting, using bigger and bolder fonts. The stock items for a shop selling electrical goods are being monitored using the spreadsheet. The cell highlighted contains a formula, not a number and can be used as a teaching point.

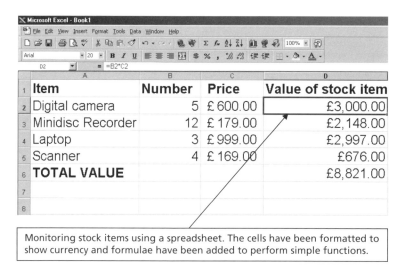

Monitoring stock items using a spreadsheet. The cells have been formatted to show currency and formulae have been added to perform simple functions.

Fig. 4.5 Screenshot from Microsoft Excel with shop example.

Evaluation/follow-up

What technical knowledge did you need to have to carry out the activity successfully?

What areas of the curriculum were supported by using the database or the spreadsheet or both?

Were there aspects of maths, for example, which could *only* have been taught using the spreadsheet or the database or both?

What was the contribution to the children's development in science when using the database?

What did you notice about the talk that was going on around the activity?

Was there evidence of children supporting and learning from each other?

Make notes which will help you to think of occasions in which ICT tools such as these provide curriculum contexts in themselves in other subjects.

Sharp, J, Potter, J, Allen, A and Loveless, A (2002) *Primary ICT: Knowledge, Understanding & Practice*. Exeter: Learning Matters.
Smith, Helen (1999) *Opportunities for ICT in the Primary School*. Stoke-on-Trent: Trentham Books.

If you feel you have successfully completed the task, return to the needs analysis table and mark it off with the date. Ask your mentor or tutor about being able to use this activity as evidence of meeting the Standards for QTS.

Chapter 4   Evaluating ICT resources

Link to Professional Standards for QTS

Paragraph 3.3.10

'Those awarded Qualified Teacher Status must demonstrate (that) they use ICT effectively in their teaching.'

Essential background

This activity builds on the activity in Chapter 3 where we considered, at a surface level, the suitability of software for purpose (see **pages 62–64**). We attempted to judge software from our own knowledge and perspective. In this activity, we will begin to look at judgements about the suitability of ICT to support subject teaching by referring to our observations of children.

Our evaluation focuses on programming tools, from floor robots to on screen logo, a set of ICT resources which have been designed specifically for use in the Early Years or primary school setting. It is important to find out how the tools allow progression in the subjects concerned and attempt to make evaluative judgements about them as learning tools in a range of subject areas.

To undertake the activity you need to be familiar with and have access to a programmable toy such as a Roamer or Pip (manufactured by Valiant and Swallow Systems respectively). These simple robots are available in many primary schools and Early Years settings. It may be that your college has one or more of them to lend out. Another possibility is the LEA ICT advisory team in your local area.

Children use these devices in the context of the subjects or learning areas listed above to explore concepts such as space, distance, direction, giving instructions, measure of angle as turn. Instructions are issued to the Roamer and Pip on a keypad on top. The instructions are issued in a specific sequence with the direction first, followed by the distance or degree of turn. This specific sequence is part of the means by which children are introduced to programming. They learn that there is a syntax associated with their commands. They have to use the language that the programmable toy understands in order to make it perform certain functions.

As a starting point with younger children it is useful to go back to their knowledge of devices or toys which they know about that require instructions in order to perform tasks. This can include their toys but also devices at home.

Children can be challenged when using these devices to estimate distance or amount of turn. They can be challenged to enter commands as a complete list, to devise ways of recording their commands. They can be encouraged to discuss their work as it progresses, developing their speaking and listening skills. Children will also have to respect both the equipment and the need to take turns and share the activity, linking to their personal and social development.

Activities with the floor robots can lead into an exploration of the on screen world of logo. There are so many versions and variants available of this software type. Some of them are part of a toolkit of software (see **page 62** for a description of this term). Some of them are targeted at younger children and contain very simple functionality (an example of this would be 2Go, part of the 2simple software package called the Infant Video Toolkit). Others, such as Superlogo or Black Cat Logo contain a high degree of functionality.

The line of development that all these learning tools have in common is from the logo concept devised by Seymour Papert. Papert proposed an online environment in which children would discover mathematical and programming concepts by having to use the correct language to communicate with the computer. Typical early versions of logo appear obstructive to the user (or even rude by today's helpful software standards!) as no help is given on errors in the commands. More recent variants support the user and help them to get started.

In on screen logo, in the earliest stages of development, instructions are issued to the computer via the keyboard and they are used to draw shapes or move the turtle in a specific direction. In this way, concepts of shape and space are reinforced, as are estimations of distance and angle of turn. The means by which the instructions are added, with a specific concern for syntax and logo's own language, lay the foundation for programming, writing web pages or constructing animation later in the child's experience. They follow directly from the concrete experience of working with the programmable toys.

You will notice the possibilities for differentiation with the programmable toys and the logo. Different degrees of challenge and different levels of recording can be suggested which meet the children's individual needs.

This activity should be carried out in a school setting with children using the toys and software described. It is best suited to smaller group work but could be adapted for whole class teaching.

Task

Design an activity for children with programmable toys or logo, which challenges them, then evaluate its success in terms of the subject areas it is supporting. For the programmable toys, and for children in the Early Years in particular, some suggestions include:

- personalising the Roamer or Pip with some suitable decoration;
- using a box as the toy's 'home', ask the children to send it home from a point in the room;
- encourage talk about the directions and the choices made.

For some children, moving along a straight line will be enough; for others, turning movements can be introduced at an appropriate learning point.

With on screen logo, some suggestions include:

- Using the commands for moving backwards and forwards – can the children measure the screen? What units are being used?
- Can children draw a square, a circle, the first letter of their first name?
- Can children be introduced to the repeat command and make patterns and shapes to order?
- Can children devise further challenges for themselves and their peers?

Evaluation/follow-up

- What areas of the curriculum were supported by using the toys or the logo? Were there aspects of mathematics, for example, which could only have been taught using the toys or the logo?
- What was the contribution to the children's development in personal and social education? What did you notice about the talk that was going on around the activity? Was there evidence of children supporting and learning from each other?
- Did the use of the toys or logo promote speaking and listening in a constructive way? How?
- Make notes which will help you to think of occasions in which ICT tools such as these provide curriculum contexts in themselves in other subjects.

Fox, B, Montague-Smith, A and Wilkes S (2000) *Using ICT in Primary Mathematics.* London: David Fulton.
Sharp, J, Potter, J, Allen, A and Loveless, A (2002) *Primary ICT: Knowledge, Understanding & Practice.* Exeter: Learning Matters.
Smith, Helen (1999) *Opportunities for ICT in the Primary School.* Stoke-on-Trent: Trentham Books.

If you feel you have successfully completed the task, return to the needs analysis table and mark it off with the date. Ask your mentor or tutor about being able to use this activity as evidence of meeting the Standards for QTS.

Chapter 4 · Making the connections between subject schemes and plans

Link to Professional Standards for QTS

Paragraph 3.3.10

'Those awarded Qualified Teacher Status must demonstrate (that) they use ICT effectively in their teaching.'

Essential background

This section focuses on a two-part planning activity exploring the ways in which the curriculum strategies in literacy and numeracy can be supported and enhanced by the use of ICT. You could choose to cover one or both strategies.

The National Literacy Strategy (NLS) and ICT
The activity below assumes that you are familiar with the structure and aims of the National Literacy Strategy and that you have read the pages which discuss the use of ICT within the Literacy Hour in Chapter 2 (see **pages 28–31**).

The National Numeracy Strategy (NNS)
The guidance for the daily mathematics lesson contained within the published National Numeracy Strategy outlines more explicit teaching opportunities for the use of ICT than the Literacy Strategy. Furthermore, there is a more flexible approach to timings within the hour, which means that the different resource levels within schools can address the issues of integration more consistently.

The opening of the daily mathematics lesson concentrates on the development of mental mathematical strategies. Children are 'warmed up' with questions relating to the learning objectives that enable them to make connections between their previously gained aspects of maths knowledge.

The National Numeracy Strategy contains detailed guidance about what to do in the middle section of the daily mathematics lesson in which children are expected to work on what is called 'the main teaching activity'. The settings for this can vary between the whole class, groups, pairs or individuals.

The final element of the daily mathematics lesson is the same as for the literacy hour. It is the plenary in which the class has an opportunity to consolidate the knowledge gained during the lesson. The teacher can identify and correct any misconceptions about particular concepts and 'summarise key facts, make links to other work and discuss the next steps' (DfEE, 1999).

The guidance available on the use of ICT suggests that it can be incorporated into most parts of the lesson and gives suggestions which are related to the level of resource provision. The opening section on mental maths can be varied in its use of resources by the inclusion of a large display monitor, electronic whiteboard or projection from an overhead projector. The same applies to the plenary where the strands of the lesson can be drawn together by the use of electronic media.

Once again, however, it is the central part of the lesson which lends itself most readily to the incorporation of ICT. ICT is broadly defined in the guidance to include all of the available audio-visual aids and, of course, calculators. For the computer, several different possible uses are described for this section of the lesson, summarised as follows:

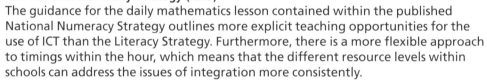

- ⮞ software to explore number patterns, including the use of spreadsheets;
- ⮞ tutorial software for practising a particular skill, with rapid assessment;

○ data handling software;

○ software for giving instructions of movement and turn in order to develop subject knowledge in, for example, measurement of distance and angle;

○ software for transforming shapes;

○ software for branching and sorting in order to develop logical thinking and problem solving.

Some of these possible uses have the potential to develop high order ICT skills. There is also a distinct overlap with items from the QCA Scheme of work for Information Technology (QCA, 1998). Given the flexible nature of the daily mathematics lesson, it ought to be possible to plan in a cross-curricular way for some of the numeracy framework. However, it is worth remembering that the focus of the lesson has to be mathematics specifically and the lesson succeeds or fails partly by the way in which the teacher can draw the class together in a plenary at the end of the session. If the activity has moved out if the realm of the initial focus and is meeting some other planning requirement, the quality of the mathematical experience will decline.

The impact of the low and high resource settings is felt in a reduced way because of the added flexibility of delivery of the numeracy strategy. However, in a low resource setting it is possible to become dependent on poorer quality courseware of a very basic drill and practice type. Where this is focused (on reinforcing a topic which is under development) and targeted (at children who need it), such software is extremely useful. As we have seen in earlier sections, where this software is used to keep certain children busy or as a reward or sanction, there is little justification for using it in pursuit of real learning objectives.

In a high resource setting, again in a network room or similar, all children could experience mathematics lessons with access to the relevant software and hardware. The whole lesson could be run in the computer suite from time to time (timetabling allowing).

The following activity could be planned away from the school environment, but needs to be carried out with children in school.

Task 1: the National Literacy Strategy

Look at the National Literacy Framework for a given year group and consider the learning objective in relation to the children you are working with.

Decide at what level of activity you could aim, according to whether you are in a high resource setting or a low resource setting. Design an activity for five or six children for the twenty minutes of group activity. Remember to consider factors such as individual school variation (some schools are evolving with the way they operate and may have longer for this part of the hour than in the original guidance). Remember also to discuss the levels of ability of the group with the class teacher and to target the actual content appropriately.

For example, if we consider one of the activities supporting learning objectives from Year 3, Term 1 for sentence level work on verbs, namely:

> '… to use verb tenses with increasing accuracy in speaking and writing, e.g. catch/caught, see/saw, go/went, etc. Use past tense consistently for narration…'

Our context from the NLS is mapped out in the analysis to the planning. For the ICT element in a low resource setting, where there is one computer to the thirty children in the class, consider getting the children to work on a pre-prepared word template file which contains, say, ten sentences with verbs in the present tense. Have a series of regular and irregular examples differentiated for ability groups through the week. Ask the children to identify the verbs in the text and change them into the past tense using the features of the word processor.

In a high resource setting, in a network room, prepare templates for the whole class, differentiated according to ability and ask them to search and replace. Alternatively, ask children to investigate the patterns in pre-prepared on screen texts and prepare a presentation about it. This is going to depend on flexibility of implementation of the strategy in the school. The context is everything. Part of analysing the situation accurately is about taking into account the school, the children, the resource setting and the relevant curriculum and strategy documents as they are being applied in that setting.

Task 2: the National Numeracy Strategy

Consider the framework for Years 1–3, for example, and look at the learning outcomes for Year 3 pupils for the Spring term – Handling Data, unit 12.

In a low resource setting, or one where the children's experience of using ICT is limited, collect simple data about the packed lunches brought to school across a given week. Ask children to enter the information and display it in data handling software. This could be done using a simple graphing tool or using a more complex data handling package.

For a medium resource setting, where there is regular access to the computer and the Y3 children have already gained experiences of simple graphing in Y2, extend their knowledge by building a more complicated database based on the different methods which children use to come to school each day.

If this is not appropriate to your needs, choose another time constrained, easily organised activity.

In either case, in your planning, develop questions which exploit the ICT learning opportunities alongside the mathematical learning opportunities

Evaluation/follow-up

Some questions to ask yourself after either task, are:

- ⮑ How was the activity integrated into the normal running of the classroom?
- ⮑ What skills did I need in order for the activity to succeed?
- ⮑ What skills did the children need?
- ⮑ How did I ensure that all children had access to the activity?
- ⮑ What were the learning outcomes for the children in literacy or numeracy respectively?
- ⮑ What were the learning outcomes for the children in ICT?
- ⮑ What assessment opportunities were there?
- ⮑ How does this experience add to my understanding of ICT in subject teaching?
- ⮑ What will I do next time?

Sharp, J, Potter, J, Allen, A and Loveless, A (2002) *Primary ICT: Knowledge, Understanding & Practice.* Exeter: Learning Matters.
Smith, Helen (1999) *Opportunities for ICT in the Primary School.* Stoke-on-Trent: Trentham Books.

If you feel you have successfully completed the task, return to the needs analysis table and mark it off with the date. Ask your mentor or tutor about being able to use this activity as evidence of meeting the Standards for QTS.

Chapter 4 — Progression, continuity and issues of assessment in ICT

<table>
<tr><td>

Link to Professional Standards for QTS

</td><td>

Paragraph 2.1b

'Those awarded Qualified Teacher Status must demonstrate (that) they have a secure knowledge and understanding of the subjects they are trained to teach … to be able to teach them in the age range for which they are trained, (and that they) have sufficient understanding of a range of work (in NC subjects including) ICT…'

</td></tr>
<tr><td>

Essential background

</td><td>

A scheme of work is intended to provide progression and a possible map of the learning of a child in a given subject. Assessment is a vital part of the process because it allows teachers to track progress and plan appropriately for children to achieve. Without proper assessment and recording in a given subject, there is no real evidence or knowledge of where the children are up to and planning becomes empty and meaningless. In the worst cases, it leads to the same activities being given out year on year to children who will underachieve because of it. In ICT this means seeing the same basic word processing activities going on at Year 6 as happened at Year 2. The planning and assessment cycle is incomplete in a school where this occurs and the children make no real progress in the subject (or in its use in other subjects)

</td></tr>
</table>

The principles which underpin good practice in assessment apply equally to ICT as a subject and ICT in subject teaching. As teachers, we are looking for ways to measure achievement which, at the same time, allow us to identify a child's learning needs. These methods of assessment, in turn, will allow us to plan efficiently and appropriately. Ways of assessing children in ICT, as in other subjects, include some or all of the following:

➲ observing how the child goes about a piece of work;
➲ diagnosing difficulties which become apparent over a series of lessons;
➲ observing which planning strategies appear to work and allow the child to succeed in a given area;
➲ collecting significant pieces of work in a portfolio of development;
➲ noting the context of the work and any factors which were significant: the grouping, the time taken, the level of concentration, etc.;
➲ noting the views of the child about the piece of work and asking her or him what made the activity so successful/significant;
➲ feeding the information back into the planning process;
➲ when appropriate, making a judgement about the child's level in terms of the level descriptions in the attainment targets for ICT in the revised National Curriculum (at the end of the Key Stages in primary schools).

At all times, a clear focus on the learning objective is very important as well as a general awareness of other learning taking place.

Nevertheless, assessment and record keeping in ICT is a complex process. Meaningful work samples are harder to come by in ICT than in many other subjects. Printouts of work by themselves, for example, have only limited use. ICT is often used as a tool to present work in its best possible light. Any revealing errors and misconceptions are often lost along the way. The finished product is only the final element of a much longer, more complex process. The process itself is what provides the real assessment opportunities. To borrow an example from another subject, English, a writing sample which contains only the finished ('best') copy is similarly without any real use. Teachers need to go back through the draft book to understand the process the child went through. The child also needs to see and understand this in order to move forward.

Some ICT tools do allow for processes to be explored. Some word processors, for example, allow changes to be tracked and printed out. Others record how many times the child accessed the online help in a particular software package. Browser software tracks the user through the various sites and links they follow. This might provide useful assessment information. Some network solutions in schools have systems which allow children to select pieces of work and store them in an electronic portfolio. Taken together, in context, these are useful tools for the teacher assessing a child's achievement and identifying their learning needs. If we add connectivity to the home computer into the equation we have a powerful, fluid record of achievement which is also accessible to parents and to children out of school hours (of course, the issue of inequality in computer and network connectivity provision in different areas becomes even more obvious in this context and will need addressing by those in control of funding).

Tutorial software, including software produced as part of an Integrated Learning System (ILS), can record the units of work which the child has covered and can produce tables, graphs and collections of statistics. These relate to the software itself and closely to the subject being taught. They are of very limited use in assessing the child's ICT capability, however, and should not usually be presented as evidence of attainment in ICT. They record particular progress through an on screen worksheet or tutorial. As we have seen in the planning chapters above, the ability to use tutorial software only demonstrates the ability to use tutorial software. True ICT capability is much more than the ability to follow on screen instructions and click on the button which says 'next' or 'continue'.

The most useful tool in assessment in ICT is the teacher's own observation of the child in all contexts and their interaction with them about their work. In all of the resource settings we have discussed in this section, this presents real logistical difficulties and requires systematic planning and the use of other adults in order that it is carried out usefully. Many schools, for example, operate an assessment week with samples being collected across the curriculum at the same time, in each class, in each half term. Extra adults are sometimes drafted in to support the class teacher in this work. Collection of ICT evidence and observation could also be planned for in this way.

However, on teaching practice, with all of the course demands being placed upon you and your mentors and tutors, any assessment activity has to be focused and manageable as well as useful. Your course requirements should spell out the number of assessments to be made of children and at what particular level in each curriculum area.

It is important to bear in mind that a further issue is the collaborative nature of ICT. It is sometimes hard to separate out the individual contributions to a joint project. There will be times when this is irrelevant and unnecessary. However, whilst collaboration itself is always to be encouraged, our school system is focused on the achievement of individuals and, at the end of the relevant Key Stages, a level of attainment must be ascribed to an individual. It becomes important therefore to develop skilled observations of individual contributions to partner work in ICT. Developing skills in monitoring the situation in this way further protects quieter, less dominant children from being overlooked.

There are relatively simple systems which you can use to track the progress of a class of children at a very basic level. Using a ticksheet (created using your table generating skills developed in the first theme in this chapter) you can record children's confidence at logging on, opening programs, saving work, using the mouse and so on.

More detailed individual profiling provides a means of systematically tracking an individual child in some detail. It is more time-consuming and you will need to focus on a representative sample of children in the class. The sorts of areas which need to be recorded include the full context in which the child was working, the curriculum context, the level of confidence and so on. At some point you will need to gain familiarity with the level descriptions in the National Curriculum.

The level descriptions, which map out progression for children in all subjects can be located at the back of the revised National Curriculum Handbook (DfEE 2000a). The level descriptions of capability for a child in any subject are intended to be applied at the end of a key stage using a judgement of 'best fit'. That is to say, the teacher reads the descriptions and decides on a numerical level on the basis of observations and knowledge of the children in the class. If, all year round, there has been a sound, formative assessment process which informs the planning, backed by samples and observations, these end of Key Stage judgements will be relatively easy to make and have a higher level of accuracy. In other words, they will be more meaningful to the child and to her or his teachers and parents.

Ideally you should attempt to observe in another class, either before or after yours, in terms of age and Key Stage. This will enable you to get an idea of progression and continuity. If children at Year 5 are doing much the same things as at Year 1 (copy typing for example), where is the progression in terms of ICT skills?

The following activity must be carried out with children in your placement school or school workplace. For children in the Foundation Stage, adaptations will need to be made to the pro forma.

Preparation
Choose two children in the class who are at different levels of attainment and observe their progress in ICT over a period of four or five weeks on at least three occasions.

Task
Complete the following pro forma (or create your own to complete).

Date			
Name of child			
IT context (computer in class/ network room, etc.)	Was the child working in the network room or on one machine. What was it?		
Software/web	Using software standalone or on the Internet		
Type (Tutorial cd, office tool, etc.)	If the child was using software, write the type here		
QCA or school unit if app.	Which QCA or school study units if any was the child using?		
Working with partner? Who?	Was the child working alone, with a peer, with the teacher, parent or other adult?		
Length of time	For how long?		
Confidence with hardware, mouse. keyboard	Rate the child's confidence with the hardware listed and/or with printers or other devices. Very, fairly, not very, needing support etc.		
Software navigation (use of menus)	As above but for navigation within the particular piece of software		
File management... saving, opening, renaming work, etc.	As above but for working with files, re-opening them, knowing where to find work etc.		
Curriculum context. Using computer to support work in English, science, maths	How was the child operating within the curriculum context? Did the computer support the subject? Were there particular difficulties? Did the use of ICT help to improve the outcome?		
Child's view of their ICT	Ask the child about their view of themselves as a user of ICT. Were there significant things about this piece of work that pleased them?		
Give best fit level if app.	Using the level descriptors, if appropriate, make a best fit judgement of the child		
Where next?	What activities with ICT would move the child forward?		

Evaluation/follow-up

Did the process enable you to assess more accurately the developing skills of the children in your class?

Did you have to make adaptations to the pro forma and to any elements of the guidance?

Did the changes improve the effectiveness of the assessment? How?

There is a longer discussion of the issues relating to assessment in **Sharp, J, Potter, J, Allen, J and Loveless, A** (2002) *Primary ICT: Knowledge, Understanding & Practice*. Exeter: Learning Matters.

If you feel you have successfully completed the task, return to the needs analysis table and mark it off with the date. Ask your mentor or tutor about being able to use this activity as evidence of meeting the Standards for QTS.

Chapter 4   Developing children's ICT skills

Link to Professional Standards for QTS

Paragraph 2.1b

'Those awarded Qualified Teacher Status must demonstrate (that) they have a secure knowledge and understanding of the subjects they are trained to teach ... to be able to teach them in the age range for which they are trained, (and that they) have sufficient understanding of a range of work (in NC subjects including) ICT...'

Essential background

In a previous activity in this theme, we looked at bringing the use of ICT much more into the world of the classroom. This was partly to develop children's awareness of the use of routines to protect their work, ensure their equal access to the computer and so on. Another aim was to develop children's independence and ICT skills in a number of basic areas:

➲ how to log on and start work at a computer;
➲ how to run software of many different kinds (tools, courseware, content-rich, etc.);
➲ how to save the many different sorts of files made with the various software tools;
➲ how to navigate to files which you have previously made and work with them again.

These basic skills are the same essential skill set required by any user of ICT and you will no doubt have encountered them yourself.

The activity described below has the purpose of reinforcing these skills and deepening understanding of a range of ICT tools. As each new software type is introduced, it should be seen for what it offers the user, for the context within which it can be used and, increasingly, how it can be used alongside other tools. There are clear connections to previous activities in this chapter where children are required to start thinking about how to bring various ICT tools and files together in a presentation or publication.

In this activity children see that there are such things as word processors and data handling programs and so on. They see that these pieces of software create files which are saved somewhere. They see that the websites they visit on the Internet can be saved as favourites to be revisited. They see that they can save their email messages. They are introduced to the idea that they can work with ICT with each of these tools in different ways, for different purposes. They learn more than this: that the essential principle for computer use is being aware of where the files are and how to work with them again and, if required, send them to others.

The activity also asks children, at the appropriate stage and during the appropriate activity, to consider peripheral devices. Various ICT tools work with the computer to acquire digital information. Here are some examples with which they will become familiar.

➲ Children will see how scanners take a 'real' image and make it into something which can be used and manipulated on the computer in a graphics package.
➲ Children will see datalogging equipment grabbing data from the environment and making it into a form which can be manipulated on screen and displayed in different ways either in bespoke software or in a spreadsheet.

⊃ Children will see how they can video discrete chunks of story or information themselves and how the computer takes this information in as a file which can be cut and pasted and altered in any number of ways. The camera, working in combination with the computer takes the real information into the digital world and makes it editable.

Other peripheral devices with which they come into contact are themselves controlled by the computer. Control boxes are used to convey commands generated by software in order to move parts of models. Like the other peripherals referred to in preceding paragraphs, children need access to control technology to widen the scope of their understanding of ICT. Units within the QCA scheme of work depend on access to this equipment (see below).

Conceptually, the activity below is about knowing that ICT creates files of different kinds. These files are pieces of digital information stored on the computer ready for manipulation, combination and communication with others. The mechanics of using the different tools is to be learned at the point of need. The most important concept after deciding on the task itself is understanding your own location within an ICT system and the location of the files which will help you to complete the task.

Finally, the activity is situated within the QCA scheme of work for ICT as a precursor to a range of tasks, each of which further subdivides and develops ICT concepts and skills.

The activity should be carried out with children in a school setting.

Task

Ask the children to think about the software that they have available on their computer and to try to describe what each title is or does. Encourage them to move towards the formal descriptions of software types. If you have a toolkit of software, ask the children to look at the ways in which the titles are described. You may find that the usual categories emerge with different language ascribed to them: word processing (something to write with), data handling (something to save information with), graphics or image handling (something to draw with) and so on. The children may also want the Internet to be included as a type of software or activity. You, or they, could helpfully break this down into email (writing to people) and browsing (looking for information).

Next, ask the children to think about a range of purposes for using the computer and then about which tools they would use for which purposes. This can be linked to the QCA scheme of work for Key Stages 1 and 2 children.

At Key Stage 1, the scheme tends to suggest activities which fall into the category of having a single piece of software or hardware which can be used. Before taking the children into the activity, encourage them to suggest tools based on what they know. In doing this, they are laying the foundations of 'fitness for purpose' which will be revisited throughout their school career with ICT.

Here are some example units from Key Stage 1 which use specific software types:

⊃ Unit 1B – Using a word bank: needs a word processor with talking word bank facility.
⊃ Unit 1E – Representing information graphically I: pictograms: needs a graphing package for producing pictograms.
⊃ Unit 2A – Writing stories: needs a word processor.

At Key Stage 2, the scheme itself suggests more than one tool for use in its activities. This is essential in developing children's awareness of ICT solutions to tasks being of more than one kind, working in combination. Here are some example units from Key Stage 2 which use more than one specific software type:

⊃ Unit 3A – Combining text and graphics: needs a graphics package, a word processor, and a collection of clip art on CD-ROM.
⊃ Unit 4B – Developing images using repeating patterns: needs a graphics package and peripheral ICT equipment such as a scanner or digital camera.
⊃ Unit 5E – Controlling devices: needs control boxes, switches and output devices.
⊃ Unit 6D – Using the Internet: needs Internet access, desktop publishing software, word processing, etc.

Carry out an age-appropriate activity with the children from the QCA scheme (or school or LEA scheme) and focus in your evaluation on the ICT concepts and skills in evidence (cross reference to assessment materials in the activity on **page 101**).

Evaluation/follow-up

How easy was it to get the children to think about the tools they were going to use for the given tasks? What did it tell you about their understanding of ICT?

Did they have access to appropriate tools? If not, why not?

What personal skills and understanding did you need for the activity to succeed?

MacFarlane, Angela (ed.) (1997) *Information Technology and Authentic Learning.* London: Routledge.
Sharp, J, Potter, J, Allen, A and Loveless, A (2002) *Primary ICT: Knowledge, Understanding & Practice.* Exeter: Learning Matters.
Smith, Helen (1999) *Opportunities for ICT in the Primary School.* Stoke-on-Trent: Trentham Books.
Somekh, Bridget and Davis, Niki (eds) (1997) *Using Information Technology Effectively in Teaching and Learning.* London: Routledge.

If you feel you have successfully completed the task, return to the needs analysis table and mark it off with the date. Ask your mentor or tutor about being able to use this activity as evidence of meeting the Standards for QTS.

C4 Children's skills

Chapter 4

Developing children's ability to make connections and solve problems

Link to Professional Standards for QTS

Paragraph 2.1b 'Those awarded Qualified Teacher Status must demonstrate (that) they have a secure knowledge and understanding of the subjects they are trained to teach … to be able to teach them in the age range for which they are trained, (and that they) have sufficient understanding of a range of work (in NC subjects including) ICT…'

Essential background

This activity builds on the previous activity which developed children's understanding of the use of ICT in the world outside the classroom.

ICT as a subject in its own right has its own set of concepts and skills. Sometimes these are difficult to separate out from the context in which they are employed. We have seen in the ICT in subject teaching how the various curriculum strategies can be supported by appropriate use of computers and Internet connections. The area of development of ICT as a subject in its own right steps outside the subject areas and curriculum strategies to engage with the issue of ICT itself.

In this case, the activity described below looks at two tasks and associated pieces of software and attempts to break them down into concept and skill sets which reflect ICT as a subject in its own right.

The activity depends on access to either a piece of presentation or desktop publishing software. The two titles which immediately spring to mind will be the Microsoft titles Powerpoint and Publisher respectively. There are alternatives to these available and all work in roughly the same way.

Presentation or desktop publishing software require similar skill sets. Both depend to an extent on gathering together material that has been created elsewhere by different applications and linking them. In the case of presentation software, text, graphics, music, movie clips and animations can be drawn together to make a presentation either of a project or a piece of work for a class, for the school, for parents, or for the Internet if required. In the case of desktop publishing software, text, graphics, word art and so on are drawn together to produce a finished publication for a variety of purposes, for a class, for the school, for parents, or for the Internet if required.

The ICT skills necessary to make either activity successful include:

➲ knowing where your various files are saved and how to navigate to them;
➲ being able to put files together using the facilities within the combining software;
➲ knowing something about the size of files and how importing them may make your end product very large in terms of storage;
➲ knowing something about the machine on which the presentation will be shown or the publication will be printed.

Many of these are higher order skills and will be demonstrated by older children. For younger children, varying degrees of differentiation will be necessary. However, the skills of young children and their vision of the overall finished product should not be underestimated or overlooked. If the end product is grasped as an idea, children will often identify where and how to go about using the tools as required.

This activity should be carried out with children at school.

Preparation

Prepare an activity which makes use of either a piece of presentation software or desktop publishing title, such as Publisher. Some contexts for the work might include a:

- ⊃ greetings card;
- ⊃ school or class magazine;
- ⊃ presentation about a particular theme or topic;
- ⊃ parents evening newsletter or presentation to run during a parents evening.

Some units in the QCA scheme of work which incorporate some of these ideas include Unit 3A – Combining text and graphics, and Unit 6D – Using the Internet.

Task

After completing the activity, make notes in the following evaluation matrix to try to analyse the ICT skills and concepts which were being developed.

Task in presentation software	ICT skill being developed	Task in desktop publishing software	ICT skill being developed
Logging on		Logging on	
Launching the software		Launching the software	
Choosing a template		Choosing a template	
Inserting a graphic		Inserting a digital image from a camera	
Finding graphic file in picture folder		Using a piece of clip art	
Inserting a music file		Choosing the right font style	
Making the slides change in an interesting way		Making the publication accessible to a wide audience	
Inserting a video clip		Selecting an appropriate printer	

If you have time you could complete an ICT skills assessment pro forma on one or two of the children (see the activity on **page 101**).

Evaluation/follow up

Were you able to carry out these activities with the children?

What personal ICT skills did you need?

What did you make of the children's ability to combine the different elements of ICT?

How did this advance your understanding of the ways in which children think about using ICT tools to complete tasks?

Smith, Helen (1999) *Opportunities for ICT in the Primary School*. Stoke-on-Trent: Trentham Books.
Somekh, Bridget and Davis, Niki (eds) (1997) *Using Information Technology Effectively in Teaching and Learning*. London: Routledge.

If you feel you have successfully completed the task, return to the needs analysis table and mark it off with the date. Ask your mentor or tutor about being able to use this activity as evidence of meeting the Standards for QTS.

For the activities you have completed in this chapter, you can use the following table to summarise your professional development. Put a line through the activities which you did not need to complete. Where you carried out an activity, rate your confidence level roughly from low to high and make any comments you feel will be useful to you.

THEMES	Developing skills Activities completed	Confidence level Low → high				Comments
ICT in planning and assessment	Using more advanced features in word processing					
	Date					
ICT in locating and using resources, including for SEN and EAL	Finding out more about school provision / Interviewing the ICT co-ordinator					
	Date					
Routine maintenance and connecting external equipment	Learning about the computer continued - basic troubleshooting and maintenance					
	Date					
Using the Internet (Becoming part of an online community for education)	Organising a web browser, searching and finding useful and usable resources for education.					
	Date					
Using ICT in curriculum subjects and in the learning areas of the Foundation Stage	Subject related examples: Using **databases** and **spreadsheets** in Maths and Science					
	Date					
Evaluating ICT resources (software, hardware, websites)	Evaluating the use of a specific learning tool (curriculum example – floor robot)					
	Date					
Making the connections between subject schemes and plans	Planning work in the schemes and strategies: Literacy and Numeracy					
	Date					
Progression, continuity and issues of assessment in ICT	Beginning to assess children's skills in ICT					
	Date					
Developing children's ICT concepts and skills	Involving children in the choice and use of a range of ICT tools					
	Date					
Developing children's ability to make connections and solve problems	Integrating tasks and integrating skills with **presentation** software and desktop publishing					
	Date					

C4 Conclusion

You have begun to develop specific aspects of your professional knowledge, understanding and skills across all the themes covered. By the end of this chapter, the combination of your reading and the classroom-based activities will have provided you with a good foundation upon which to build. It is essential that you check that you have evidence to support all the statements within the needs analysis table at this level and you have also cross-referenced this to the standards required for QTS. It is important to talk to your teacher about your progress at this stage. They will also be able to help you check that you do have appropriate evidence to audit your progress against the Standards. However, you will also need to ensure that you have started to complete the profiling required by your training provider since this may cover additional Standards.

You are ready to move on to the activities in Chapter 5, Extending your Skills.

Chapter 5   **Extending your Skills** ⊃ Introduction

Contents

The activities in this section are aimed at people who have become confident at using ICT in their personal and professional development, in subject teaching and as a subject in its own right. The emphasis in this section will be on refining knowledge and skills and on putting them together to create new levels of use and understanding of ICT in education.

The work described in this section can be carried out in a range of settings. As before, for this strand of development, most activities can be carried out at your own pace, in your own time wherever you choose to do them.

Generally, the work described in the strands of ICT in subject teaching and ICT as a subject in its own right should be carried out in school with access to appropriate hardware and software and, on occasion, to appropriate Internet connections. There are, as before, occasions when it may be possible or even desirable to do these activities at home or college. In order to help you make a judgement about where each activity may or may not be most suitably carried out, as before, each activity description contains a series of hints that suggest where it could be carried out.

For the purposes of auditing your development during your training, each strand of development is linked to a Professional Standard for QTS As you complete each piece of evidence, you can ask a mentor or visiting tutor to sign to say that this has been achieved and it can then be added to your profiling. Each training provider will approach this in different ways and it is important to link completion of the tasks in this book to the profiling requirements of your training.

The activities in this chapter are arranged as follows:

Themes	Page reference	Activity title	Area of Development
ICT in planning and in assessment	Page 113	Collecting and making use of data and information from websites	PERSONAL AND PROFESSIONAL USE OF ICT. (cf QTS standards 2002, para 2.5)
ICT in locating and using resources, including for SEN and EAL	Page 115	Exploring additional provision for children with SEN and EAL	
Routine maintenance and connecting external equipment	Page 118	Learning about peripheral devices for capturing and storing images	
Using the Internet (Becoming part of an online community for education)	Page 120	Joining an online community for education	
Using ICT in curriculum subjects and in the learning areas of the Foundation Stage	Page 122	Using ICT in the foundation subjects	ICT IN SUBJECT TEACHING. (cf QTS standards 2002, para. 3.3.10)
Evaluating ICT resources (software, hardware, websites)	Page 128	Evaluating Internet resources/being aware of safety issues	
Making the connections between subject schemes and plans	Page 130	Combining different subject areas with ICT/using ICT in the Learning Areas of the Foundation Stage	
Progression, continuity and issues of assessment in ICT	Page 133	Issues of continuity and progression	ICT AS A SUBJECT IN ITS OWN RIGHT. (cf QTS standards 2002, para. 2.1 b)
Developing children's ICT concepts and skills	Page 135	Evaluating teaching and learning with ICT	
Developing children's ability to make connections and solve problems	Page 137	Using webpage authoring or hypermedia with children	

As before, each activity is outlined in full and has the following information provided with it:

⊃ link with the ICT National Curriculum and/or the QCA scheme of work for ICT (if applicable);
⊃ link to another subject in the National Curriculum or to its related strategies (for this example, where relevant);
⊃ QTS skills test link (if applicable);
⊃ note of the possible audit point against the Professional Standards for QTS;
⊃ essential background to the activity including such items as which equipment to use and which setting might be most appropriate for carrying it out;
⊃ description of the activity and all the elements which go to make it up;
⊃ some ideas on how to evaluate its success;
⊃ finally, some suggested further/background reading.

Chapter 5   ICT in planning and assessment

Link to Professional Standards for QTS

Paragraph 2.5:

'Those awarded Qualified Teacher Status must demonstrate (that) they know how to use ICT effectively, both to teach their subject and to support their wider professional role.'

Essential background

This activity presumes that you have undertaken the word processing activities in Chapters 3 and 4, and that you are familiar with downloading resources from websites.

Some websites, which are useful as a background to this activity, are listed and described below:

OFSTED – www.ofsted.gov.uk
The OFSTED website contains complete lists of OFSTED publications and inspection reports. Most of these are in a form that can be downloaded. You can navigate an alphabetical list of Local Education Authorities and find the report for the school in which you are placed and read it. It could be useful to you when searching for a job or for a school for your children. You can even read about your training provider's performance in their most recent OFSTED inspection. The methodology for these is entirely different to school inspection. Again, you can read about this on the OFSTED site.

It is worth bearing in mind that there is a 'sell-by' date on OFSTED reports beyond which they no longer accurately reflect the school. It is possible that a school with either a poor or a positive report could have subsequently changed direction. Factors such as staff and pupil turnover in the two or three years after inspection are highly significant. Use the OFSTED site as a port of call and as one part of an overall view of a school. You will need to visit to establish a more up-to-date view.

The Standards site – www.standards.dfes.gov.uk
This is a sub-section of the Department for Education and Skills (DfES) website and contains lots of information about the performance of schools. The infamous 'league tables' of SATS results for the end of Key Stage 2 are here (specifically at www.dfee.gov.uk/performance/primary_00.htm#tosearch). These provide some indication of the performance of a school which could be useful in regard to forming a view. Certainly if you look here for information and at OFSTED and carry out a visit, you will have a much clearer picture. Remember, that all of these pieces of evidence are only a partial picture in themselves, useful only when seen in their proper social context. Graphs which show how a school's results have altered over time are available at the statistics part of the DfES website at www.dfes.gov.uk/statistics

BECTA – www.becta.org.uk
This is the British Education and Communications Technology Agency website. This is for anyone who is interested in learning more about the impact of ICT on teaching and learning. It has many thousands of pages of links to research, areas for feedback and discussion about ICT in education.

QCA – www.qca.org.uk
The Qualifications and Curriculum Authority maintains this website which contains information about the school curriculum and its assessment. It is linked to a site that illustrates progression at www.ncaction.org.uk

NGfL – www.ngfl.gov.uk

This is the homepage of the National Grid for Learning, which contains many links to resources on the Internet for education, including policy documents and other government websites. A link on the homepage takes you straight through to an alphabetical listing of resources for education, which is sometimes the quickest way to find anything on any government site.

The sites listed above are a few of the many government sites for education.

Quoting links in printed text is always risky because web pages have a habit of moving. All the resources listed have established themselves and are likely to remain in some form for the foreseeable future. If a name change occurs, typing the link will usually result in you being pointed automatically to the new site. Failing that, a search engine will find the relevant government site for you.

This activity can be carried out at home or at school or college, and wherever you use a computer with a reliable Internet connection.

Task

For this activity, you need to carry out the following elements and make notes on how you went about it.

You need to open up a word processor and type a heading 'About the school' and save it as a file 'Report to parents'. Next, minimise it so that it is running in the background.

1   Visit the OFSTED website. Locate the most recent report for the school in which you are placed or working at the moment. Download it to your computer. You will need to run Adobe Acrobat to read it. Usually it runs automatically in your Web browser window and takes it over in order to display the report for you. With the report showing in the window on screen, browse to the 'Main findings of the inspection', usually near the beginning. Using the text selection tool select the paragraph headed 'What the school does well' and copy it. Move to your word processor window and paste it into the document you are creating there.
2   Next, visit the Standards site and locate the performance data for your school using the link above. Highlight the text and the graph of SATS scores for the last four years. Again, copy and paste this into your file on the school.
3   Write some text that links these two pieces of information together about how well the school is performing.
4   Begin a new section in your report to parents about the school's use of the Internet. You are going to reassure parents that the safety aspects have been considered. You will need to visit the National Grid for Learning pages (using the link above) and visit the area on safety, which is available from the homepage.
5   Copy and paste relevant sections and link them with a short piece of text demonstrating that you have considered aspects of children's safety when using the Internet.

Evaluation/follow-up

Which aspects were difficult for you?

If you find that it was manipulating the windows so that you could use your word processor and the other pieces of software at the same time (Web browser, possibly Adobe Acrobat Reader), then you need to practise multi-tasking generally.

If you were unable to locate the resources then you may need to ask for help or check that the links are still valid. This would be a good collaborative activity with a fellow trainee or teacher.

Visit the websites above to gain useful background information. See also the websites listed in the bibliography.

If you feel you have successfully completed the task, return to the needs analysis table and mark it off with the date. Ask your mentor or tutor about being able to use this activity as evidence of meeting the Standards for QTS.

ICT in locating and using resources

Link to Professional Standards for QTS

Paragraph 2.5:

'Those awarded Qualified Teacher Status must demonstrate (that) they know how to use ICT effectively, both to teach their subject and to support their wider professional role.'

Essential background

Special Educational Needs
Children who have Special Educational Needs (SEN) can be supported by the targeted use of ICT, both hardware and software. For many children with SEN, ICT forms a part of their Individual Education Plan (IEP) and, depending on the local context and the needs being addressed, ICT solutions are sometimes funded fully for individuals.

Some examples of ICT used to support learners with SEN include:

➲ software which addresses the needs of a dyslexic child;
➲ hardware which allows access to the computer for a child with motor impairment;
➲ browser windows which open up in larger fonts for visually impaired children;
➲ portables or laptops with specialist software loaded for very particular needs (this might include one specialist device or laptop assigned to one child in particular);
➲ specialist hardware for those who are using wheelchairs, such as specialist keyboard mounts or switching devices;
➲ software and hardware adapted for visually impaired children;
➲ software and hardware adapted for hearing impaired children.

Some companies are dedicated to finding solutions for access for children with SEN and they will welcome enquires about their software and suggestions for future development. They are usually smaller companies who depend on a close relationship with the schools and children with whom they work. The annual British Educational Technology and Training exhibition (known as the BETT show) includes a Special Needs Village for you to examine at first hand such solutions. Furthermore, the website for the BETT show remains online all year round and contains a searchable directory of educational ICT suppliers, including for SEN. Another very good source of information on SEN issues is the BECTA website and the activity which follows will make use of their 'inclusion' pages.

For children with SEN in your class it is important to discover if they require any additional access to the computer in the form of hardware that makes it easier to point and click at menu items or enter text. Some examples include:

➲ Concept keyboard – a device which allows touch sensitive areas to be created on a flat A4 or A3 board which can be set up to input particular items of text or commands. Teachers can tailor the concept keyboard to the particular needs of an individual child using authoring software provided. The software also includes printing facilities.
➲ Touch window – a device which attaches to the front of a monitor allowing the user to touch areas of the screen as a replacement mouse click to gain access to the menus in given software.
➲ Big keys – a larger format keyboard for children with fine-motor-control difficulties.

⊃ Switches – on/off rack mounted switches for wheelchair users and others, which equate to left and right mouse clicks.
⊃ Trackballs – large inverted mouse systems where the user is able to move a larger ball over a bigger area to point and click.
⊃ Small mice – smaller point and click devices for smaller hands with motor-control difficulties.

In terms of software for SEN, there is a very wide range indeed. Most of it can be used to access the curriculum including the units of work in the ICT scheme of work by means of levelled menus and different screen setups. Many word processors for children in the primary school allow you to create customised user levels.

One example of targeted software use is for children who have dyslexia or language delay. Titles that are widely used in this case include Wordshark and Numbershark and you may well find these in your placement school.

For both hardware and software, you also need to be aware of any technical knowledge that you require to operate the equipment successfully.

English as an additional language
As children with English as an additional language (EAL) begin to acquire more English, the computer, if properly managed, allows them to experiment with forms of written and spoken English in an unthreatening and motivating environment. Some additional tutorial software may be appropriate but talking word processors can be just as effective with immediate feedback provided on composition. The biggest benefit is in areas where the child can experiment with open-ended software alongside peers.

Community languages with their own alphabets and letter systems are available through specialist software, such as Globalwriter, or as font add-ons in office software. These can be used to produce signs and instructions in the appropriate language. In turn, this goes some way to demonstrating that the home language of the child is valued in the context of the school.

For younger children in this context, sensitive adult intervention and peer support are crucial. There should be plenty of opportunity to try to move conceptual development along by talk in the home language alongside support for learning English.

The choice of software should include elements that allow for the child to choose menu items by pointing and clicking, to have sections of text spoken, to allow access to pictures music and video. Multimedia authoring packages can be useful in this context. There is enormous potential for producing home-grown resources in dual language format. This would be an exciting project for Year 6 for the Multimedia Authoring Unit. Resources could be created for any age in the school by the older children asking parents, siblings, other adults to help to record in the home language.

Organising ICT for children with EAL carries the same responsibilities and requirements as for organising any area of the curriculum for them, namely:

⊃ never assume the level of language learning – find out;
⊃ differentiate for levels of English appropriately; do not assume that all EAL learners are the same or have the same learning style;
⊃ make sure that EAL children understand all the processes involved in switching on and off, logging on and off and saving work;
⊃ check and re-check understanding with sensitive questioning.

In terms of investigating different languages and cultures in our classrooms, the Internet provides many useful resources. One example is the 'I love languages' website (www.ilovelanguages.com) which opens up a huge number of links to cultural websites, languages and alphabets from all over the world, translation sites and more.

The following activities should be carried out at the placement school. However, some of the research elements can be carried out at home or in a college setting.

There are two tasks and the detail of their completion will vary according to the setting in which you are working.

Task1: Investigating ICT provision for SEN

a) Interview the ICT co-ordinator and/or the SEN co-ordinator (SENCO) about ICT in your school which is being used for/by children with SEN. Ask about the following issues:

➲ Which special educational needs are being supported by ICT in the school?

➲ Choose two examples, preferably different sorts of needs, and answer the following questions:

➲ Is the support in the form of additional hardware or software to allow access to the computers?

➲ Is the support in the form of specialist software to meet a specific learning difficulty?

➲ What other kinds of needs are being met and how?

➲ What does the class teacher need to know in order to use the ICT equipment or software SEN successfully?

b) Following on from the above, or if you find that there are no examples for you to use in your particular setting, visit the BECTA inclusion website. Locate case studies and examples of children using ICT to address:

➲ a specific learning difficulty; and

➲ a physical access issue which means that they require adaptations to existing equipment.

Follow this with a visit to the BETT show website and investigate suppliers of hardware and software which will address these particular needs. Make any notes that you feel are useful to help you to repeat this activity in your professional role as a teacher when you have your own class.

Task 2: Investigating ICT provision for EAL

a) Establish the range of community languages spoken in the school in general and in your class specifically. You might do this by talking to specialist teachers of EAL children at the school, or the class teacher or one of the senior managers. In some schools there are co-ordinators for children for whom English is an additional language. Having identified the range of languages and the individual needs of the children concerned, discover from the class teacher or ICT co-ordinator which ICT resources, if any, are used to support their learning of English and their learning in other subjects.

b) Following on from the above, or if you find that there are no examples for you to use in your particular setting, visit the 'I love languages' website. Research the resources on the Internet that are available to support the particular languages and cultures represented in the school in general and in your class in particular. Make any notes that you feel are useful to help you to repeat this activity in your professional role as a teacher when you have your own class.

Evaluation/follow-up

➲ How easy was it to locate resources for your SEN children within the school?

➲ Did you find that there were technical considerations in using specialist resources?

➲ If there were no specialist resources for SEN was it easy to make adaptations to existing resources?

➲ Did you find that the websites provided you with useful information in an accessible form?

➲ For your EAL children, if applicable, was it easy to locate specific software types or websites being used with them?

➲ Did you find that the websites provided you with useful information in an accessible form?

SEN

The websites in the text:

The BECTA inclusion site – follow the links from www.becta.org.uk
The BETT show website – follow the links to the search pages at www.bettshow.com

Some software suppliers have very interesting pages with useful background on SEN and inclusion and ICT. Search for Widgit, SEMERC and Clicker on the Internet, using Google or Ask Jeeves.

EAL

Websites such as www.ilovelanguages.com

If you feel you have successfully completed the task, return to the needs analysis table and mark it off with the date. Ask your mentor or tutor about being able to use this activity as evidence of meeting the Standards for QTS.

Chapter 5 — Routine maintenance and connecting equipment

Link to Professional Standards for QTS

Paragraph 2.5

'Those awarded Qualified Teacher Status must demonstrate (that) they know how to use ICT effectively, both to teach their subject and to support their wider professional role.'

Essential background

The use of external equipment to capture and record images, both still and video is being used as an example of peripheral equipment generally. Three types of equipment are being considered and it is to be assumed that you have access to one or more of them.

Digital cameras and video provide a rich medium for the act of record keeping and observation in all years of the primary school. In the hands of young learners themselves they have huge potential to develop the curriculum. For teachers of very young children – where so much of what is produced or goes in is, in may ways, ephemeral – digital media provide a way of recording and assessing progress which has not been possible before.

Digital cameras

Digital cameras are more widely available in schools through the NGfL funding, various supermarket loyalty schemes or interested parents and friends groups. They are extremely variable in quality and price and in the range of connections to the computer.

Many of the cameras store digital images on an internal hard disk. After the pictures are taken they are downloaded to the computer via a cable. No one really enjoys connecting cables to computers so many cameras feature a one-off connection. A cradle is provided which is permanently attached to one of the ports on the rear of the computer (the USB port – with which you are familiar, see page 53). After each batch of photos is taken, the camera is placed in the cradle and the images are transferred. Some of these cradles also feature a charger so that the camera may be recharged while it sits there.

Many teachers prefer to use a camera that takes a floppy disk (such as the Sony Mavica range) rather than one which uses a cable. The camera records to disk and the disk is simply placed in the drive. The images are then copied across.

One major advantage over traditional cameras is that there is no developing cost. There is, of course, the cost of the ink used to print out the images, if a printed copy is required. However, this is outweighed by the multiplicity factor. Many people can have access to the same few images that are useful on each set of shots. They can be printed, copied, emailed or stored on the local computer. They have applications in the social context of the school; they illuminate school reports and letters home. They can be used extensively on school trips or longer school journeys. They also provide a useful function in displays of work and, as mentioned above, in record keeping and assessment.

For schools that prefer to stick to traditional photographic equipment, sometimes on the grounds of superior image quality, there is still the potential to have electronic copies of images from some film developers. Some high street companies will copy images to CD at the point of developing them. These can then be accessed from the school computer.

Digital Video Cameras

Many of the same uses apply to the digital video (DV) camera. The ease with which clips of children's activities and performance can be transferred is justification alone for many of the schools beginning to get involved with this use of peripheral image devices. The possibility of video used to disseminate good practice with a DV camera as the medium of transfer is another justification.

At the time of writing this technology is restricted to newer computers or those which have been expensively adapted to allow for the transfer of the video. You may recall that in the first activity in this theme in 'Getting Started' we looked at Firewire connections. These are required for ease of use. Once the video clip has been downloaded, there are specialist software tools required on the computer.

The Apple corporation has been spearheading the use of digital video on their iMac and iBook computers by selling them already set up to work with DV cameras. All new iMacs and iBooks come with the ports needed for transfer and with software called iMovie. This allows for easy combinations of clips and effects, which look professional. The latest versions of iMacs include the facility to create DVD versions of the movies made with children. BECTA has been investigating the use of such technology with children and the website will be reporting on ways of using them (www.becta.org.uk).

Scanners

If you need to convert photographs that have been taken or if you want to have digital versions of children's original pieces of work, a scanner is a useful peripheral. The most common kind used in the school or in the home resembles the top part of a photocopier. There is a lid and when this is raised there is a glass plate underneath. The image is placed underneath and software at the computer is used to generate a scan. The scanner converts the image into something usable onscreen.

In terms of connections, scanners connect to a whole range of ports at the back of the computer. The one at school will already have been set up. You could ask the ICT co-ordinator or technician (if there is one) to show you where the scanner is connected. Often, more recent scanners are connected to the USB port.

This following activity can be carried out at home with your own camera or video equipment or scanner or at school.

Task
Using one of the pieces of technology listed in the first part of this section, learn how to transfer a small video clip or small set of pictures to the computer. This could be a record of a visit to a school or an outing on which you went with the children.

Put the images or clips into an appropriately labelled folder on your computer. You can make use of them in later activities in this chapter.

Write notes to help you to remember how to go about connecting and using peripheral equipment for working with images and video.

Evaluation/follow-up
➲ How easy was it to carry out? Did you have to rely on the manual or were you able to obtain support from teachers or colleagues on the course?
➲ Have you managed to download still pictures or video clips into appropriate folders?

Visit the BECTA website for information about digital video in the curriculum: www.becta.org.uk, including the ongoing pilot projects in schools.

For further information on digital cameras, make use of the How Stuff Works website at www.howstuffworks.com

If you feel you have successfully completed the task, return to the needs analysis table and mark it off with the date. Ask your mentor or tutor about being able to use this activity as evidence of meeting the Standards for QTS.

Chapter 5 Becoming part of an online community for education

Link to Professional Standards for QTS

Paragraph 2.5

'Those awarded Qualified Teacher Status must demonstrate (that) they know how to use ICT effectively, both to teach their subject and to support their wider professional role.'

Essential background

This activity asks you to think about how you might use the Internet to join an online community of fellow professionals. Some advantages of this include the opportunity to:

- ➲ share resources and expertise;
- ➲ share issues and how they might be overcome; and
- ➲ receive help on particular issues of locating resources (or simply getting ideas).

The activity first asks you to look into this at a local level.

The NGfL was envisaged as a place within which 'structured discussion' between teacher professionals would take place. The activity goes on to ask you to investigate such facilities with the NGfL or within your college context.

This activity can be carried out at home, in a college network room or in your placement school.

Task: the online forum element of the Internet

In the first instance, see if your colleagues would be interested in setting up a mailing list to share ideas and practice. This could be very useful if you are on a long practice or placement and geographically dispersed from each other. You need to establish some parameters carefully at the outset and create the right kind of culture of exchange of ideas.

Secondly, ask your training provider whether or not they provide any element of your course online. Also, find out if your LEA training provider has an online component. If neither of these parties has any online discussion element, visit the Virtual Teachers Centre at the NGfL (follow the link) and explore the online forums that are available in a subject or area of your choice.

Make notes – or download a manual – which explain the features of the discussion forum or online environment. Answer, in your notes, the following questions.

- ➲ Can you send email to just one person?
- ➲ How do you use the noticeboard facility?
- ➲ Can you publish to your own area?
- ➲ How do you use the discussion areas?
- ➲ Is there a chat room and how do you access it?
- ➲ Is there a statement of safety and etiquette for using the environment?
- ➲ Can you log in from anywhere on the Internet?
- ➲ How do you know when new messages have been posted?
- ➲ Are the discussion areas moderated?

Evaluation/follow-up

Were you able to enter any discussions of curriculum issues with ICT in any of the online forums available?

Are they well used? What kinds of exchange have been most useful?

DfEE (1997) *Connecting the Learning Society*. London: DfEE.
DfES (2002) *Transforming the Way we Learn*. London: DfES.

If you feel you have successfully completed the task, return to the needs analysis table and mark it off with the date. Ask your mentor or tutor about being able to use this activity as evidence of meeting the Standards for QTS.

Chapter 3

Using ICT in curriculum subjects and in the Foundation Stage learning areas

Link to Professional Standards for QTS

Paragraph 3.3.10:

'Those awarded Qualified Teacher Status must demonstrate (that) they use ICT effectively in their teaching.'

Essential background

This activity is for trainees on placement in Key Stages 1 and 2, or for interested Foundation Stage trainees to complete.

There is a great deal of pressure of time in the primary school day on the core curriculum subjects of mathematics and English. However, with imaginative organisational strategies and access to the appropriate hardware and software, it is possible to find opportunities to use ICT in subject teaching in the Foundation subjects.

Art and design
At Key Stage 1, while children are being taught about 'visual and tactile elements, including colour, pattern and texture, line and tone, shape, form and space' they can use painting software to explore some of these elements (*Art & Design, Knowledge & Understanding, KS1 4a* in DfEE, 2000a).

At Key Stage 2, the use of digital and video cameras to record observations is suggested as part of the strand on exploring and developing ideas (KS2, 1c). There is also a recommendation that children are encouraged to create material for a school art gallery on the school webpage.

A powerful suggestion is made about the use of the Internet as a medium for children exploring the work and styles of many different genres across the world. This will depend as always on the accessibility of reliable and fast Internet connections, such as those promised by Broadband technologies (cf. The 'Using the Internet' theme in Personal and Professional Use of ICT) in which teachers, children and trainees find themselves. Nevertheless, these are possibilities which are unique to ICT and which significantly enhance the teaching of the subject. With bandwidth and distribution of the Internet around schools improving all the time, virtual art galleries represent a significant contribution to the art and design curriculum. The higher bandwidth (much faster transfer of much bigger files around the Internet) is of particular benefit in this area because the files are so much larger than with other uses of ICT, for example, word processing.

In terms of planning appropriately, the usual judgements apply about how the subject is enhanced and which ICT skills are being utilised and developed. There will be further discussion of this issue in the themes in the area of development of ICT as a subject in its own right. However, you can find connections between art and ICT in the ICT scheme of work, and could usefully situate your ICT content within the art curriculum. Units such as 1A (An Introduction to Modelling) 2B (Creating Pictures), 2C (Finding Information), 3A (Combining Text and Graphics) and 6A (Multimedia Presentation) are all areas that can be approached from the direction of ICT and taken into the area of art and design.

Similarly, it is possible to find examples within the QCA scheme for art that are rich with possible links to ICT. Unit 2A, Picture This!, for example, suggests a unit of work around children recording an issue or event in their lives which 'could also link with

Unit 1A "An Introduction to Modelling", in the ICT scheme, when children create their own representations of real or fantasy situations' (Scheme of work for art).

Purposeful exploration of painting packages, image recording devices and websites which bring art into the classroom in ways which were not possible before are all unique to ICT and offer something back to children's learning in art and design. The important thing to remember for your planning is the word 'purposeful' and all that implies. Of particular importance is the notion that the ICT is adding to the potential achievement and learning by the children in the given subject.

History and geography

History and geography are two subjects in which ICT can make a contribution to the enhancement of the learning process.

For geography, the Internet puts many resources within reach. The subject itself offers a context for developing skills of searching, emailing and publishing. Similarly, early understanding of mapping and routes is enhanced by the use of a programmable toy. Other possibilities include using a digital camera to record images of the local environment and bringing them back for discussion and use with hypermedia or web page authoring tools, or using the Internet to obtain comparative weather information.

Beyond comparative weather data, comes the whole series of possibilities raised by email contact with children and teachers in other localities. Emailed questions about what you can see from your window on a given day generate vast amounts of interesting information between pupils of the same age, across the world, very quickly. One example of this kind of project was in the Lambeth Connections Project (formerly the Brixton Connections Project, now at www.lambeth-connections.org.uk).

Geographical resources that were not available before – detailed maps and aerial photographs of most of the world – are now accessible on CD-ROM and Internet. The skill in terms of the teaching will be to integrate the use of these resources usefully into planning. You will need to identify opportunities for learning that are uniquely offered by the technology and then allow your pupils to have access to it.

History is brought to life by many of the activities suggested in its own scheme of work for the primary school. The opportunities for ICT are present throughout. The Internet brings not only art galleries into the school, but also museums and archival resources of all kinds. Many of these are also present on CD-ROM. Incorporating such work into history lessons, as with all subject areas, becomes an issue depending on the resource setting in which trainees, teachers and children are working.

Curriculum 2000 makes several references to links between history and ICT. Some of these are simply to the resource capabilities of ICT as for example the link to finding out about significant people in the past from CD-ROM (link to statement 4a on Historical Enquiry).

Higher order ICT skills are demanded by the sophisticated use of databases at Key Stage 2 to study patterns of change over time. This falls in the following area for history:

> *'(the capability to)ask and answer questions, and to select and record information relevant to the focus of the enquiry' (Historical Enquiry, 4b).*

History provides us with an example of the need to be very clear about the sort of order of skills in both a curriculum subject and ICT that are to be developed in a given lesson.

Design and technology

ICT offers much to teachers of design and technology in primary schools. The area of most potential is probably that of control technology where children learn that they can control devices and models that will respond to instruction and inputs from outside. Children already know that such devices exist. A quick brainstorm at the start of work on this subject will bring to mind video recorder programmers, washing machine programmes, central heating timers, burglar alarms and a whole host of other devices.

Additionally when creating or developing ideas for themselves, children could be encouraged to create digital versions of their ideas. The programmes of study make explicit reference to this idea, pointing out the link back to ICT in the following statements:

Pupils should be taught to:

a) generate ideas by drawing on their own and other people's experiences
b) communicate their ideas using a variety of methods, including drawing and making models.
(From KS 1, Strand 1: Developing, planning and communicating ideas.)

At Key Stage 2 there is a greater level of complexity and a more explicit statement of the need to engage with ICT in order to deliver the subject. There is a further statement about the tools of presentation and onscreen creation available through ICT (cf., again Strand 1: Developing, planning and communicating ideas). There is, however, an understanding that in developing a knowledge and understanding of materials and components.

Pupils should be taught:

c) how mechanisms can be used to make things move in different ways, using a range of equipment including an ICT control program.
(From KS2, Strand 4: Knowledge and understanding of materials and components.)

It is difficult to imagine being able to meet the needs of young learners in design and technology and their curriculum entitlements without significant levels of ICT use in their school career. Again, the major caveat is whether the resource base is high enough in your placement school to begin exploring this issue in your planning.

A further issue is the availability of support in terms of expertise. Although relatively simple to use, specialist software and hardware is involved and there is something about the number of wires and additional interface boxes involved which deters many people from including this area in their planning. Most teachers that do plan for it find that the equipment and software working together is highly motivating for children and stimulates a great deal of interest and creative learning potential.

Music
ICT has for a long time enjoyed a close relationship with music in primary schools. Tape recorders and CD players have been used in schools for many years to:

⮕ bring children into contact with music from different times and different cultures;
⮕ record children's own compositions;
⮕ provide resources for learning songs;
⮕ provide accompaniment to dance (link to PE);
⮕ provide a source of music for assemblies and performances; and
⮕ provide a resource for budding instrumentalists to record and assess their work.

Additionally, schools with electronic keyboards have been able to extend the performance aspects of assembly songs. Keyboards with sound modules in which real instrument voices have been stored allow children to explore the different timbres and possibilities of different instruments.

In terms of computer use, there are software packages available which allow children to explore composing. The feedback that they gain from such software is immediate and the 'performing and appraising' aspects of the curriculum are therefore made similarly immediate. As with art and design, there is no suggestion of the computer-based musical tools replacing hands-on experience with the whole range of instruments found in primary schools. Instead, the suggestion is that ICT be used to enhance the learning process.

Children learn that computers are capable of storing more than just text and images but that they can be used to record and manipulate sound. To put it another way, they learn that sound itself can be represented and stored digitally in which form it can be transformed in many different ways.

Computers and hard disk recorders are now the medium of choice in professional and home recording studios for composing and arranging music. Children will be aware of the possibilities of mixing and remixing songs as they hear different versions of their favourite songs produced. The learning curve for teachers and others who are seeking to use music composition software and keyboards at this higher level is quite steep and requires specialist training. However, once the basic concepts are mastered, such devices open up a whole range of possibilities for young composers in both key stages, but particularly the older ages in Key Stage 2 in the primary school.

The links between ICT and the programmes of study for music are many and can be found in statements such as:

2. Pupils should be taught how to:
a) create musical patterns
explore, choose and organise sounds and musical ideas.
(From KS1, Creating and developing musical ideas – composing skills.)

There is a further link with the concept of sound exploration:

3. Pupils should be taught how to:
make improvements to their own work.
(From KS1, Responding and reviewing – appraising skills.)

And, finally, a link to the use of recording equipment for reviewing work (this could be tape or computer based).

The Breadth of Study for Key Stage 2 in music requires that children use ICT to 'capture, change and combine sounds.'

RE, PSHE and citizenship

ICT in terms of its access to resources on the Internet is a major contributing factor to growing subject knowledge and understanding in the inter-linked areas of religious education (RE), Personal, Social and Health Education (PSHE) and citizenship. The diversity of religions over the world can be explored on the Internet and on CD-ROM. Children can have a context for their writing which extends their sphere of personal expression into that of personal belief.

The RE scheme of work links with ICT in many places. Two examples would be: in the unit on Belief and Practice (Unit 1D, where it mentions the resourcing possibilities) and also in Unit 4D on 'What religions are represented in our neighbourhood?'

This time, there is more to be made of the capacity of ICT for preparing and representing writing. Digital cameras and the Internet are suggested means of gathering and storing information about local faiths, which are then to be represented in children's classwork.

One extremely useful resource, which groups together hundreds of RE websites from faiths and cultures all over the world, is at www.allre.org.uk

As for history and RE, the potential of the Internet to link to other cultures and belief systems can engender respect (when taught appropriately). ICT brings these worlds within reach (with all the caveats about connectivity and appropriate Internet use) in a unique way.

For the non-compulsory areas of PSHE and citizenship, there are statements of usefulness of ICT in the revised National Curriculum. One example is that of developing relationships through work and play: for example, communicating with children in other countries by satellite, email or letters.

ICT also has a part to play away from the machinery itself in the wider discussion about ethics. The sorts of issues in the standards with which trainees would be engaging in work of this kind include those listed in 18C: ethical issues – including:

> *i access to illegal and/or unsuitable material through the Internet;*
> *ii acknowledging sources;*
> *iii data confidentiality;*
> *iv the ways in which users of information sources can be (and are) monitored; and*
> *v material which may be socially or morally unacceptable.'*

Some of these issues are discussed further in activities later in this chapter.

It is as well to raise the issue of ethics in its widest sense with older... will be aware of the fact that not everyone has access to computers and that the World Wide Web as a phrase refers to circumnavigation rather than connectivity in all countries. Access to websites which map cyberspace will be particularly revealing in this regard. One example would be the Institute of Cybergeography which has a fascinating collection of atlases of cyberspace (at www.cybergeography.org).

Physical education

There is a place on the physical education (PE) curriculum for ICT at least in terms of devices that can help to record movement for pupils to analyse later. Some schemes of work are distributed for school training using different storage and replay media, whether it is on videotape or videodisc.

Previously, PE was excepted from the list of subjects in the 1995 version of the National Curriculum in which children were expected to develop their ICT capability. The revised National Curriculum is altogether more enthusiastic and stated linkage with ICT includes the following:

⊃ For Dance and Gymnastic Activity at Key Stage 1, 'Pupils could use videos of movements and actions to develop their ideas.'
⊃ For Dance, Gymnastic and Athletic activities at Key Stage 2 'Pupils could use video and CD ROMs of actions, balances and body shapes to improve their performance.'

Further cross-curriculum opportunities exist in the analysis of the effects of exercise, which can be carried out using sensors. Here, the potential link to science has already been outlined above. The potential to link with mathematics in the exploration of data in spreadsheets is also clearly there. Some bespoke software exists to do this (the 'Five Star' athletics software, for example).

Clearly, it would be unwise to make strong claims for all day, every day pervasive links in planning between ICT and PE. However, there will be times, particularly when tackling the issue of assessment in PE, when ICT can make a vital contribution.

ICT and Foundation subject planning aid

The table below gives you locations of some example units in the various QCA schemes of work for the Foundation subjects with strong links to ICT. It also links the ICT scheme of work back to that subject. The list is not exhaustive. It is intended as a guide for planning from whatever scheme of work document you may have access to in order to incorporate ICT in that subject. There are certainly many other links between the various schemes of work.

Foundation subject	Subject scheme of work: Example units with links to ICT	ICT scheme of work: Example units with links back to the subject
Art and Design	Picture This (2A) Investigating pattern (3B) People in action (6A)	An introduction to modelling (1A) Creating Pictures (2B) Multimedia Presentation (6A)
Geography	Improving the environment (Unit 8) Investigating rivers (Unit 14) The mountain environment (Unit 15)	Combining Text and Graphics(3A) Multimedia Presentation (6A) Using the Internet...(6D)
History	How did life change in our locality in Victorian times? (Unit 12) How can we find out about the Indus Valley civilisation? (Unit 16) What can we learn about recent history from studying the life of a famous person? (Unit 20)	Combining Text and Graphics(3A) Analysing data (5B) Using the Internet...(6D)
Design and Technology	Packaging (3A) Lighting it up (4E) Alarms (4D)	Finding Information (2C) Combining Text and Graphics(3A) Controlling Devices (5E)
Music	Journey into space: exploring sound sources (unit 18) Songwriter exploring lyrics and melody (unit 19)	Manipulating sound (3B) Multimedia Presentation (6A)
RE, PSHE and Citizenship	Beliefs and Practice (1D) Celebrations (2C) What religions are represented in our neighbourhood? (4D)	Finding Information (2C) Email (3E) Using the Internet...(6D)
PE	Dance activities – unit 1 Gymnastic activities – unit 5	Finding Information (2C) Monitoring environmental conditions and changes (5F)

The following activity can be carried out at school and/or at home.

Task

Choose a subject from amongst the Foundation subjects, which is to feature in the scheme of work for your class.

Identify a unit of work. Cross-reference it to an ICT unit from the ICT scheme (with which you will be familiar from other activities in this book). Use Table 22 to help you. Decide on the balance between the two and plan a series of 4–6 lessons (or activities) that develop the subject knowledge of the children alongside some identified aspect of ICT capability.

Evaluation/follow-up

At the end of the sequence, address the following issues as an overview of all the sessions:

Were the learning objectives achieved? How?
Which aspects of ICT capability did the children develop (not rehearse, but develop)?
What operational difficulties were encountered (if any) during the activity?
Make a judgement, in conversation with your mentor and/or tutor, about the contribution of the ICT to the subject knowledge in the sessions.
Did the ends justify the means? Once again, consider the time factor.
Would you use ICT to work with this particular concept or unit again?
If yes, would you do anything differently?
If no, why would you prefer not to use ICT in this way again?

DfEE (2000a) *National Curriculum Handbook for Key Stages 1 and 2*. London: DfEE.
Sharp, J, Potter, J, Allen, A and Loveless, A (2002) *Primary ICT: Knowledge, Understanding & Practice.* Exeter: Learning Matters.
Smith, Helen (1999) *Opportunities for ICT in the Primary School*. Stoke-on-Trent: Trentham Books.
Somekh, Bridget and Davis, Niki (eds) (1997) *Using Information Technology Effectively in Teaching and Learning*. London: Routledge.

If you feel you have successfully completed the task, return to the needs analysis table and mark it off with the date. Ask your mentor or tutor about being able to use this activity as evidence of meeting the Standards for QTS.

Chapter 5   Evaluating ICT resources

Link to Professional Standards for QTS

Paragraph 3.3.10

'Those awarded Qualified Teacher Status must demonstrate (that) they use ICT effectively in their teaching.'

Essential background

This section includes two activities to help you consider:

1 a basis for reviewing Internet Resources; and
2 the safety issues around using the Internet.

You can find a fuller discussion of these topics in Chapter 2 **pages 25–27**.

Internet resources

As with any area of resourcing there is a need for evaluating the usefulness and usability of Internet resources. There is already a huge variation in terms of the quality of production of such materials, from the ubiquitous 'worksheets' through to the more complex lesson plans. The activity in 'extending your skills' sets out a possible framework for review which takes into account the main issues confronting the end user: cost, quality, relevance, accessibility and more.

Safety on the Internet

Schools must have a policy on the Internet in their school called an Acceptable Use Policy and they must have informed parents about the use of the Internet in the school. The policies and the letter are produced by the school and its governors and are written to provide a mechanism for dealing with safety issues.

The activity below will ask you to investigate how access to, and regular use of, the Internet is organised to address safety issues. It can be carried out at home, in a college network room or in your placement school.

Task 1: Evaluating resources

Visit one of the following educational resource sites:

- Educate the Children at www.educate.org.uk
- The Channel Four Education site at www.4learning.co.uk
- The Primary Resources site at www.primaryresources.co.uk

Search for a resource for teaching your age group in literacy or numeracy. Evaluate its usefulness against the following criteria:

Web resource review sheet (fill in what you can!)	
Title of web resource:	
Address of webpage from where it is linked:	
Subject area(s):	
Key Stage(s):	
Any relevant National Curriculum or Scheme of Work link:	
Any relevant special educational needs opportunities:	
Is the resource essentially a downloadable paper-based piece of work?	
or, is the resource making use of the computer and features of the Internet?	
1. Access: Is the site free or is it a subscription site?	
2. Content and curriculum relevance: As far as you know, does the content appear to be relevant to the National Curriculum programmes of study and strategies? To which subject or learning area and in what ways?	
3. Design and navigation: Is the design clear and uncluttered?	
4. Ease of use: Are all of the features easy to use? Does the site require extra software in order to make full use of it?	
5. Conclusion: Would you recommend this site to your colleagues?	

Task 2: Safety on the NGfL

Visit the safety website following the link from the NGfL homepage. Download and print an example Acceptable Use Policy. Does it address items on the following checklist?

- ⮑ curriculum possibilities of the Internet (a rationale for using it in the first place);
- ⮑ an acknowledgement of some risk factors;
- ⮑ access by the children;
- ⮑ access by teachers, parents and other adults;
- ⮑ email addresses and how they are managed;
- ⮑ how access to the Internet is filtered for safety reasons;
- ⮑ how concerns can be raised; and
- ⮑ children's photographs on the school website.

Make any notes which will be useful to you when you are working with children in your own class on the Internet.

Evaluation/follow-up
- ⮑ What elements of technical knowledge did you need to have before undertaking any of the activities?
- ⮑ Did you gain an understanding of the range of websites available for teachers?
- ⮑ Did you gain an understanding of the safety issues of working on the Internet with children?

Meeting the QTS Standards

If you feel you have successfully completed the task, return to the needs analysis table and mark it off with the date. Ask your mentor or tutor about being able to use this activity as evidence of meeting the Standards for QTS.

Making the connections between subject schemes and plans

Link to Professional Standards for QTS

Paragraph 3.3.10

'Those awarded Qualified Teacher Status must demonstrate (that) they use ICT effectively in their teaching.'

Essential background

These two activities look at how ICT can be used in a cross-curricular setting in Key Stages 1 and 2 and in different learning areas of the Foundation Stage. Choose which of these activities is most applicable to your current placement or work setting.

Key stages 1 and 2 cross-curricular issues

With the concern over standards of writing nationally, the National Literacy Strategy is making much more of cross-curricular opportunities than before. It is worth spending some time considering how to use ICT in the teaching of English in a cross-curricular sense. Beyond the structure of the literacy hour, children use English in the following ways:

- ⮑ publishing a science write-up;
- ⮑ creating a local area guide book in geography;
- ⮑ writing school webpages;
- ⮑ generating a historical account;
- ⮑ writing about their beliefs in recreating rules for classroom and playground behaviour in PSHE;
- ⮑ generating captions to explain findings in mathematical data handling;
- ⮑ reading for information in any of the Foundation subjects, science and mathematics.

The issue for planning for ICT to support these wider uses of English is, as usual, how to operate in the differing resource settings and differing cultures of ICT in schools.

Higher resource settings are going to allow for much greater exploration of the provisional nature of information, simply because faster, more distributed Internet access through a school means that greater numbers of teachers and children can become involved.

In lower resource settings, where one computer is still shared between the class, there are still opportunities for engagement with the wider English curriculum. The TTA commentary on the subject (*Using ICT to meet teaching objectives in English*, TTA, 1999) describes examples from speaking and listening (encouraging children to defend choices made in simulations and adventure games), reading (whole class reading sessions from the screen) and writing (using the word processor as an aid to drafting materials and understanding the writing process better).

The cross-curricular opportunities for developing English outside the literacy hour are many and varied and the limit to what is feasible will be determined largely by the children's access to software and hardware.

Think about a curriculum area in which you are expecting the children to write at the computer (it could be one of the topics listed above).

The Foundation Stage
For those working in the Foundation Stage, you need to make a thorough assessment of the opportunities for ICT according to the parameters established in the discussion on **pages 21–24**. See the alternative activity listed below.

The activity can be carried out partly at home or college, and at school during its implementation.

Task 1: cross-curricular ICT: English, geography and ICT
Create a lesson plan which focuses on the specific areas of development of the writing itself which you are developing using the ICT.

Give a lesson overview that describes the English element, the ICT element and the element from the other subject. For example, a lesson overview for 'Creating a local area guide book in geography' for Year 4 might describe the ICT element as using desktop publishing software and digital images. The geographical element could be from the work on localities described in the revised National Curriculum (see below). The English element is the developing sense of audience and of how to present information in a clear and accessible manner.

Describe in your plan the school/class context, the learning needs of the children and the grouping/timing. Don't forget to describe the resource setting for ICT in the school.

In order to resource the activity properly, make the most of information collected on local area trips, in particular, digital images, video clips and sound recordings which could be incorporated into the work on the computer. Consider working with a multimedia authoring package to produce a multimedia version of the guidebook if you are fortunate enough to be in a highly resourced setting.

Note the context of the National Curriculum:

An example for ICT could be from 'Finding Things Out' at Key Stage 2 – pupils should be taught how to 'Prepare information for development using ICT …'

For geography from the programmes of study for KS2 – In their study of localities and themes, pupils should: 'study at a range of scales – local, regional and national …'

For English from the programmes of study for KS2 – The range of purposes for writing should include: 'to inform and explain, focusing on the subject matter and how to convey it in sufficient detail for the reader …'

Record the context of the scheme of work, for example, for ICT: QCA Unit 4a.

For English, see the NLS Units for Y4, for Geography, see the Scheme of Work… etc.

Make notes, which will be useful to you, under these headings.

- Your own learning needs
- Organisational memory joggers
- Other adults you may have to help you – what are their roles during the lesson?
- Learning objectives
- Differentiation
- Learning needs – EAL (English as an additional language)
- Learning needs – SEN (Special Educational Needs)
- Assessment opportunities
- Key questions
- Lesson format
- Evaluating the lesson part 1 – operational issues
- Evaluating the lesson part 2 – learning outcomes
- Evaluating the lesson part 3 – next time

Task 2: Foundation Stage
Choose one of the Learning Areas of the curriculum for the Foundation Stage.

Identify, with the help of the Early Years team at the school, an appropriate piece of software with which the children are already familiar. Set the computer up within some kind of role play context if possible (if space allows and if it fits with the current planning in the setting.) Observe the children working with the software over a period of a few days for a few minutes each day. Ask for one or other of the co-workers in the setting to do the same. Collate your observations.

Evaluation/follow-up

⮞ How has the presence of the computer assisted in generating talk around the area of learning?

⮞ Have you been able to observe any interactions in which peer learning was evident?

⮞ Did the children work in the ways in which you expected?

⮞ Were there any surprising outcomes?

⮞ Were there any overlapping areas of development from the other Learning Areas?

DfEE (2000a) *National Curriculum Handbook for Key Stages 1 and 2.* London: DfEE.

DfEE (2000b) *Curriculum Guidance for the Foundation Stage.* London: DfEE.

Meadows, J and Leask, M (eds) (2000) *Learning to Teach with ICT in the Primary School.* London: Routledge.

Passey, Don *et al.* (1997) *Improve your use of IT in Teaching.* Dunstable: Folens..

Sharp, J, Potter, J, Allen, A and Loveless, A (2002) *Primary ICT: Knowledge, Understanding and Practice.* Exeter: Learning Matters.

Smith, Helen (1999) *Opportunities for ICT in the Primary School.* Stoke-on-Trent: Trentham Books.

If you feel you have successfully completed the task, return to the needs analysis table and mark it off with the date. Ask your mentor or tutor about being able to use this activity as evidence of meeting the Standards for QTS.

Chapter 5 Progression, continuity and issues of assessment in ICT

Link to Professional Standards for QTS

Paragraph 2.1b

'Those awarded Qualified Teacher Status must demonstrate (that) they have a secure knowledge and understanding of the subjects they are trained to teach ... to be able to teach them in the age range for which they are trained, (and that they) have sufficient understanding of a range of work (in NC subjects including) ICT ...'

Essential background

Having gained some insight into individual children's performance in ICT in the previous activity in this theme (**pages 99–102**), it is important to consider the wider picture across the school in order to refine your understanding of progression and continuity in ICT in the primary years.

In order to look across the school you will need to be able to spend some time observing children out of phase, that is to say, outside of your normal age range. You will recall that we discussed the issue of progression in the previous section on assessment and in the background to the whole scheme of work for ICT. The scheme of work in the school (whether it is the QCA scheme or an LEA scheme or a school scheme), backed by thorough assessment, ought to prevent the children from being asked to do substantially the same activities in ICT at the age of ten as they were at the age of six.

Children who were led through the process of opening a piece of work in, say, a word processor, at the age of seven should, by the time they are eleven, be much more independent in their working.

The QCA defines characteristics of progression that can be used to provide a context for your observations of children in different age phases:

⊃ Level 1 – Using ICT to explore options and make choices to communicate meaning. Pupils develop familiarity with simple ICT tools.
⊃ Level 2 – Purposeful use of ICT to achieve specific outcomes.
⊃ Level 3 – Using ICT to develop ideas and solve problems.
⊃ Level 4 – The ability to combine and refine information from various sources. Pupils interpret and question the plausibility of information.
⊃ Level 5 – Combining the use of ICT tools within the overall structure of an ICT solution. Pupils critically evaluate the fitness for purpose of work as it progresses.
⊃ Level 6 – increased integration and efficiency in the use of ICT tools. A greater range of complexity of information is considered.

(Source www.qca.org.uk – abstracted from the level descriptions in the *National Curriculum Handbook*, (DfES, 2000a)).

For children aged seven at the end of Key Stage 1, the expectation is that they will be operating at least at level 2. For children aged 11 at the end of Key Stage 2, the expectation is that they will be operating at least at level 4 and above.

The following activities should be carried out in school.

Task

In order to gain some idea of continuity and progression in your school setting observe the children in another setting out of your normal age phase. Choose two children who are at different stages of ability and complete an observation pro-forma. Use the pro-forma from the activity on **page 101** or a similar one of your own devising. Compare the strategies that the children employ in this setting.

➲ Is there evidence that their knowledge, skills and understanding in ICT are being developed across their time at the school?
➲ What is enabling them to do this?
➲ Is it a change in expectations? What else may be playing a part?
➲ Are the activities progressively more demanding? In what ways are they more demanding?
➲ Do they enable children to develop their thinking skills and their ability to make connections and solve problems?

Make notes that will be useful to you in addition to completing the pro-formas on the children.

Evaluation/follow-up

➲ Were you able to match up expectations in the various National Curriculum documents, schemes and handbooks with what you could see in school? In what ways were there differences?
➲ Were you able to gain a clearer understanding of the issues of progression and continuity in ICT?

DfES (2000a) *The National Curriculum Handbook*. London: DfES.
The QCA website (www.qca.org.uk).
The National Curriculum in Action website (www.ncaction.org.uk).

If you feel you have successfully completed the task, return to the needs analysis table and mark it off with the date. Ask your mentor or tutor about being able to use this activity as evidence of meeting the Standards for QTS.

Link to Professional Standards for QTS

Paragraph 2.1b

'Those awarded Qualified Teacher Status must demonstrate (that) they have a secure knowledge and understanding of the subjects they are trained to teach … to be able to teach them in the age range for which they are trained, (and that they) have sufficient understanding of a range of work (in NC subjects including) ICT …'

Essential background

This activity requires that you become aware of some exemplification of children's developing ICT skills and concepts. As you will have seen if you have completed the activity on Issues and progression in ICT (**pages 133–134**), the QCA sets out a model of progression through six levels, drawn from the level descriptions in the *National Curriculum Handbook*, (DfEE, 2000a).

As a map of children's developing concepts and skills, this can only become useful in the context of either your own observations or some kind of exemplification. The latter can be provided by the activity below which requires that you set these in the context of the exemplification provided by the National Curriculum in Action website (www.ncaction.org.uk). The activity below suggests that you look closely at exemplar material there and follow it with reflection on your own work with your own class.

The activity can be carried out at home or college as appropriate.

Task
Visit the National Curriculum in Action website. Locate an ICT activity within your age phase and explore it as a resource, using the following questions as a guide.

- ➲ What skills in ICT are in evidence from the children's work?
- ➲ What work had to be carried out in advance?
- ➲ How does it compare with the levels of ability which your children are exhibiting?
- ➲ Are there elements of the work which are similar to activities which you have carried out?

Think of a lesson you have carried out in ICT that had a major input on ICT as a subject in its own right. Use the following questions for your activity and the example lesson from the National Curriculum in Action website (answering only those elements which you can know for certain).

- ➲ How was the activity integrated into the planning in the other subjects?
- ➲ What skills were needed in order for the activity to succeed?
- ➲ What skills did the children need?
- ➲ How did all children have access to the activity (or was it for a select few only)?
- ➲ What were the learning outcomes for the children in ICT as a subject in its own right?
- ➲ What assessment opportunities were there?
- ➲ How did this experience add to your understanding of ICT in subject teaching?
- ➲ What will you do next time?

Evaluation/follow-up
- ➲ What conclusions can you draw from the activity?
- ➲ Are your expectations set at a similar level to the exemplar activities?

The NC action website listed above.

DfEE (2000a) *National Curriculum Handbook for Key Stages 1 and 2*. London: DfEE.

DfEE (2000b) *Curriculum Guidance for the Foundation Stage*. London: DfEE.

DfEE (2000c) *Information and communication technology: Scheme of work for KS1 and 2*. London: DfEE.

If you feel you have successfully completed the task, return to the needs analysis table and mark it off with the date. Ask your mentor or tutor about being able to use this activity as evidence of meeting the Standards for QTS.

Chapter 5 | Developing children's ability to make connections and solve problems

Link to Professional Standards for QTS

Paragraph 2.1b

'Those awarded Qualified Teacher Status must demonstrate (that) they have a secure knowledge and understanding of the subjects they are trained to teach … to be able to teach them in the age range for which they are trained, (and that they) have sufficient understanding of a range of work (in NC subjects including) ICT …'

Essential background

These activities build on the activities for this theme in Chapters 3 and 4, where real and work-related examples of ICT were discussed and software tools were used which combined ICT resources into a final 'real' product. In this case, the activity described below looks at two possible tasks and associated pieces of software and attempts to break them down into concept and skill sets that reflect ICT as a subject in its own right.

The activities depend on access to a multimedia authoring tool such as Hyperstudio or to a Web authoring tool such as Microsoft Front Page or similar.

Hypermedia authoring and webpage authoring require similar skill sets. Both depend to an extent on linking together material that has been created elsewhere. This material, in the form of files anywhere in the system could be text, graphics, music, movie clips and animations.

The ICT skills necessary to make either activity successful include:

⊃ knowing where your various files are saved and how to navigate to them;
⊃ being able to put files together using the facilities within the combining software;
⊃ knowing something about the size of files and how importing them may make your end product very large in terms of storage; and
⊃ knowing something about the machine on which the finished product will be shown.

They also depend on a growing awareness of the need to compose resources in a different way. Unlike the previous activity in this theme, which was working towards a linear piece of work – a magazine or a presentation with a beginning and a middle and an end – this activity requires the production of a small hypermedia resource or linked collection of webpages.

As children view more webpages, CD-ROMs or other hypermedia resources they are developing as consumers of resources with many possible paths or hopping off points. It is true that a presentation or a magazine can be viewed in whole or part and that an audience can choose to an extent how to progress through it. What sets hypermedia and Web authoring apart is that they are designed with choice in mind at the outset. The reader may visit whichever parts of the resource or story they choose from the moment they visit the opening screen.

The design process for making webpages or hypermedia is predicated on the properties of the medium, just as the presentation or the publication were in the previous activity. In this case, however, the tools which are chosen actually encourage thinking about literacy and thinking about the needs of the audience in a completely new way.

There is some acknowledgement of this in the QCA scheme of work at Year 6 where the unit called 'Multimedia Presentation' requires engagement with ICT in a different way to other units. Here the content-free multimedia authoring package can be used to 'communicate and present information in music, art, history, geography, science, design and technology' (DfEE, 2000c).

These activities ask you to consider the skills needed in terms of ICT concepts. These are age appropriate again and build on prior knowledge and attainment. For Web design this means more than just the knowledge of where files are in order to put them together. It means bringing up with children the issue of their own Web experiences. For example:

➲ Which websites work well?
➲ Which are frustrating and full of graphics and animation that take a long time to load in your Web browser? Why do they take so long?
➲ Can we talk with children about connection speed and about the size of files which they will build into their Web resources?

They will need to develop a sensibility to audience in terms of the design and the appearance of a website but in terms of the ICT knowledge, they will need to make allowances for their audience's technology.

Similarly, making a hypermedia resource of interlinked pages containing animation, video, graphics and so on depends on a knowledge of how that resource will be physically presented on their audience's computer. If it has become very large because of its component parts, how will it be shared? So many ICT concepts and skills are bound up in these discussions and are introduced into the activity described below.

The activity outlined below consists of making a small number of interconnected webpages or a small hypermedia resource. It will be dependent upon your access to the available software.

With young children you will need to take account of their ability to work with different media and it is quite likely that you will physically put the resource together. With older children there is nothing in either Web authoring or creating hypermedia which should be beyond their capability. If they have had experience of creating and saving files in a wide range of software, and if they are comfortable with navigating through their user area in order to find them again, the tools in modern hypermedia software or Web authoring tools will not be beyond them.

In terms of their developing ICT skills we are working at the higher end of the scale but well within the parameters set out in the programmes of study for ICT at Key Stages 1 and 2. In terms of assessment at level 4, a child aged ten, of average ability, is expected to be able to combine and refine information from various sources.

The activity could be carried out in any setting although there would be greater benefits from working with children and hypertext.

Task
The activities consist of making a small number of interconnected webpages or a small hypermedia resource either for or with children. Link the work to a particular theme, preferably in a content-rich Foundation subject or in science. The work can take place over a period of weeks in parallel with the work in the subject itself.

➲ Decide on the audience for the webpages or hypermedia resource.
➲ Decide on the project.
➲ Brainstorm the areas that the children will work on.
➲ Divide the work into teams.
➲ Provide a diagrammatic representation of the pages and the links.
➲ Consider design issues by comparison with webpages and CD-ROMs with which the children are familiar.
➲ Raise connection and file size issues with them if it is an issue in your setting or in the setting in which your audience will view the resource.
➲ Pilot the resource with another class or group and make any refinements that are necessary.

Evaluation/follow-up

➲ Were you able to carry out these activities with the children?

➲ What personal ICT skills did you need?

➲ What did you make of the children's ability to combine the different elements of ICT?

➲ How did this advance your understanding of the ways in which children think about using ICT tools to complete tasks?

DfEE (2000c) *Information and Communications Technology: Scheme of work for KS1 and 2*. London: DfEE.
Sharp, J, Potter, J, Allen, A and Loveless, A (2002) *Primary ICT: Knowledge, Understanding & Practice*. Exeter: Learning Matters.
Smith, Helen (1999) *Opportunities for ICT in the Primary School*. Stoke-on-Trent: Trentham Books.

If you feel you have successfully completed the task, return to the needs analysis table and mark it off with the date. Ask your mentor or tutor about being able to use this activity as evidence of meeting the Standards for QTS.

For the activities you have completed in this chapter, you can use the table below to summarise your professional development. Put a line through the activities that you did not need to complete. Where you carried out an activity, rate your confidence level roughly from low to high and make any comments you feel will be useful to you.

Themes	Extending skills Activities completed	Confidence level Low → high				Comments
ICT in planning and assessment	Collecting and making use of data and information from websites					
	Date					
ICT in locating and using resources, including for SEN and EAL	Exploring additional provision for children with SEN and EAL					
	Date					
Routine maintenance and connecting external equipment	Learning about peripheral devices for capturing and storing images					
	Date					
Using the Internet (Becoming part of an online community for education)	Joining an online community for education					
	Date					
Using ICT in curriculum subjects and in the learning areas of the Foundation Stage	Using ICT in the Foundation Subjects					
	Date					
Evaluating ICT resources (software, hardware, websites)	Evaluating Internet Resources/being aware of safety issues					
	Date					
Making the connections between subject schemes and plans	Combining different subject areas with ICT/Using ICT in the Learning Areas of the Foundation Stage					
	Date					
Progression, continuity and issues of assessment in ICT	Issues of continuity and progression					
	Date					
Developing children's ICT concepts and skills	Evaluating teaching and learning with ICT					
	Date					
Developing children's ability to make connections and solve problems	Using webpage authoring or hypermedia with children					
	Date					

You have begun to develop specific aspects of your professional knowledge, understanding and skills across all the themes covered. By the end of this chapter, the combination of your reading and the classroom-based activities will have provided you with a good foundation upon which to build. It is essential that you check that you have evidence to support all the statements within the needs analysis table at this level and you have also cross-referenced this to the Standards required for QTS. It is important to talk to your teacher about your progress at this stage. They will also be able to help you check that you do have appropriate evidence to audit your progress against the Standards. However, you will also need to ensure that you have started to complete the profiling required by your training provider since this may cover additional Standards.

You are ready to move on to the final chapter, Moving on, and the final evaluation of your ICT development at this stage.

Evaluating your development

The closing section of the book is all about looking back at the way you have developed in all the themes in the three areas of personal and professional use of ICT, ICT in subject teaching and ICT as a subject in its own right.

You will probably feel confident in some areas and still in need of some development in others. You may find, for example, that while your overall confidence has increased with some themes to do with personal and professional use of ICT, you still need to look at learning about the use of video and digital images. In ICT in subject teaching, for example, you might find that you still need to do more about integrating ICT into the daily maths lesson. In ICT as a subject in its own right, you might need to engage in further study of web pages and hypermedia.

Use the following table to record any notes on completion of the activities in the themes in the three preceding chapters. If there are any areas for further development this table will help you to identify them. Remember, as always, to talk the issues over with any or all of the following, as applicable and appropriate:

- ➲ your tutor;
- ➲ your class teacher–mentor;
- ➲ your school-based tutor;
- ➲ your trainee colleagues.

Area of development	Themes	Final evaluation notes/further development where necessary
PERSONAL AND PROFESSIONAL USE OF ICT (see the QTS standards 2002, para 2.5)	ICT in planning and assessment	
	ICT in locating and using resources	
	Routine maintenance and connecting external equipment	
	Becoming part of an online community for education	
ICT IN SUBJECT TEACHING (see the QTS standards 2002, para. 3.3.10)	Using ICT in curriculum subjects and in the Foundation Stage learning areas	
	Evaluating ICT resources	
	Making the connections between subject schemes and plans	
ICT AS A SUBJECT IN ITS OWN RIGHT (see the QTS standards 2002, para. 2.1 b)	Progression, continuity and issues of assessment in ICT	
	Developing children's ICT concepts and skills	
	Developing children's ability to make connections and solve problems	

Further professional development

Your further professional development in the use of ICT in your teaching life will be driven by training priorities in your own school in the coming years. It will also be driven by your own interest level. If you have found that you have become interested in some of the issues in ICT in education and have enjoyed your experiences with computers and children, you may want to be an ICT co-ordinator. In this case, some further training will be necessary. You will also need to look at some of the reading suggested in the bibliography which follows.

The evidence you collect throughout your training year can be used to begin your professional development record. This should record your progress, performance and professional development needs, which will be reviewed on an annual basis through the performance management process. This process is one aspect of a DfES initiative to encourage and support teachers in continuing to update and share their knowledge, skills and practice in order to enhance children's learning. The DfES has provided a framework which maps the different standards that apply at different stages of a teacher's career. It also includes ten dimensions of teaching and leadership which exist within a school and you are encouraged to chart your progress against these as you move through your career. It is important for you to recognise your areas of expertise and achievements as well as identifying your development needs.

Your further training options include:

➲ NOF training (if it is still available in your area);
➲ post-NOF training (under development, so watch this space);
➲ local LEA advisory team courses;
➲ personal development, taking further exams and qualifications;
➲ a master's degree module from your local university;
➲ learning to use specific resources, e.g. iMovie, through the Apple Teacher Institute;
➲ working with commercially produced material (for example Keybytes for Teachers from Summerfield Publications or the INTEL Teach to the Future material).

You might also wish to join one or other of the professional associations. ACITT – Association for ICT in Education – is one example.

It is certainly worth visiting the websites listed alongside the further reading. You will find regularly updated resources and information from governmental and non-governmental sources. You will find other teachers out there willing to share ideas and explore similar issues with you.

At school you may find that your class is already making significant use of the Internet in Education. If you want to take this further you could, with permission, join in with one of the free online environments for school. Grid Club is one example (see Bibliography). In such projects, children and teachers make the link with the world outside the classroom and collaborate on exciting activities.

Further research and development in ICT in education is regularly reported on the Internet. You could investigate the link between ICT and 'Standards' through the IMPACT2 project (see, as noted elsewhere, www.becta.org.uk/research). You could look at innovative use of computers and a whole range of creative projects at the Ultralab website (www.ultralab.co.uk).

Finally...

You are joining the profession at an exciting stage in the use of computers and associated equipment in education. At its best, ICT will support huge leaps of imagination and development from the children in your care. They need you to be there with them, guiding and inspiring them but also showing that you are learning alongside them. Use of ICT in education changes and challenges the old relationships in teaching and learning and, ultimately, transforms the whole process. Hopefully, some of the activities in the book have helped you to grow in confidence during your training year and you will want to take ICT further as you develop your skills and confidence in your teaching career.

Glossary

This Glossary contains a few items mentioned in the text and is just a starting point. There are many more detailed glossaries on the Internet and in various published self-help guides (such as *The Rough Guide to the Internet*). There are also websites which take you through the basics of how particular pieces of equipment work in a user friendly way. One of the best known of these is at www.howstuffworks.com If you wondered what a USB port was for example (just one of many acronyms beloved of those who devise and build the ICT we use) you could do worse than look it up on How Stuff Works. There you will find words written for the non-expert and very good photographs and illustrations.

ADSL	Asynchronous Digital Subscriber Line. A way of connecting to the Internet which is faster than dialup access but makes use of existing telephone lines.
Bookmarks	Addresses for websites stored in the Netscape web browser.
Broadband	Refers to any high speed Internet access over ADSL or cable or other means quicker than a standard phone line or ISDN.
Browser	A piece of software which reads web pages and displays them on your computer.
Cable	A way of connecting to the Internet which is faster than dialup access with a modem. It uses a cable modem and a specialist ISP.
Dialup	A way of connecting to the Internet using a modem to dial up to an ISP each time you want to connect.
Download	Obtain a file or software from a website, bringing it to your own computer.
DSL	Digital Subscriber Line. This refers to all forms of digital subscription services to the Internet including ADSL.
Email	Electronic mail – best thought of as a way of sending messages to someone's pigeonhole on the Internet ready for collection. There are ways of communicating in real time but email usually works asynchronously.
Favourites	Addresses for websites stored in the Internet Explorer web browser.
Hardware	The physical machinery of ICT.
Homepage	The main starting page for any website.
HTML	Hyper Text Mark-up Language. The main language used to write web pages. Browsers make sense of HTML and display what the language tells them to.
Hyperlink	A piece of text which is heightened in some way from the text that surrounds it (usually underlined). When you click on it you move to another part of a file or to a new file or web page.
Instant Messaging, ICQ, IRC	These are ways of using the Internet to communicate in real time with another user. You need a good Internet connection and special software. It is to be used with extreme caution in schools, if at all, because of the potential risks involved.
ISDN	Integrated Services Digital Network. A way of connecting to the Internet which is faster than standard dialup.
ISP	Internet Service Provider
Menu	A list of choices which drops down when you click on something.

Modem	A device that connects to the phone line and allows your computer to dial another one. Sometimes these are internal, sometimes external.
PPP	Point to Point Protocol. The means by which your computer connects to another one over a phone line.
RAM	Random Access Memory. The memory which a computer uses to run software.
ROM	Read Only Memory. The memory which is used to store files and software.
Software	Applications such as Windows or Office which run on a computer and perform various tasks.
URL	Uniform Resource Locator. A technical term for a website's address. www.bbc.co.uk is the URL for the BBC website.

Bibliography

Government publications and guidance

DfEE (1997) *Connecting the Learning Society*. London: DfEE.
DfEE (2000a) *National Curriculum Handbook for Key Stages 1 and 2*. London: DfEE.
DfEE (2000b) *Curriculum Guidance for the Foundation Stage*. London: DfEE.
DfEE (2000c) *Information and communication technology: Scheme of work for KS1 & 2*. London: DfEE.
DfEE (2000d) *Using ICT in the Daily Mathematics Lesson*. London: DfEE.
DfES (2001*) Statistics of Education: Survey of Information and Communications Technology in Schools 2001* (Issue no. 09/01). London: DfES.
DfES (2001a) *ICT in the Literacy Hour: Whole Class Teaching**. London: DfES (*CD ROM plus small amount of written guidance).
DfES (2002) *Transforming the way we learn*. London: DfES.
DfES/TTA (2002) *Qualifying to Teach: Professional Standards for Qualified Teacher Status and Requirements for Initial Teacher Training*. London: DfES/TTA.
DfES/TTA (2002a) *Handbook to accompany the Professional Standards for Qualified Teacher Status and Requirements for Initial Teacher Training*. London: DfES/TTA.

Further reading on ICT in education: a selection

Ager, Richard (2000) *The Art of Information & Communications Technology for teachers*. London: David Fulton.
Beynon, John and MacKay, Hughie (eds) (1993) *Computers into classrooms: More questions than answers*. London: Falmer Press.
Crook, Charles (1996) *Computers and the Collaborative Experience of Learning*. London: Routledge.
Ferrigan, C (2001) *Passing the ICT Skills Test*. Exeter: Learning Matters.
Fox, B, Montague-Smith, A and Wilkes S (2000) *Using ICT in Primary Mathematics*. London: David Fulton.
Freedman, T (2000) *Managing with ICT*. London: Hodder.
Harrison, Mike (1998) *Co-ordinating information & communications technology across the primary school*. London: Falmer Press.
Kennedy, A (2001) *The Rough Guide to the Internet*. London: Rough Guides.
Kurta, John (1999) *Computers and Primary Mathematics*. London: BEAM.
MacFarlane, Angela (ed.) (1997)*Information technology and Authentic Learning*. London: Routledge.
McBride, Peter (1998) *The Schools' Guide to the Internet*. Oxford: Heinemann.
Meadows, J and Leask, M (eds) (2000) *Learning to Teach with ICT in the Primary School*. London: Routledge.
Passey, Don *et al.* (1997) *Improve your use of IT in Teaching*. Dunstable: Folens.
Sharp, J, Potter, J, Allen, A and Loveless, A (2002) *Primary ICT: Knowledge, Understanding & Practice*. Exeter: Learning Matters.
Smith, Helen (1999) *Opportunities for ICT in the Primary School*. Stoke-on-Trent: Trentham Books.
Somekh, Bridget and Davis, Niki (eds) (1997)*Using Information technology effectively in teaching and learning*. London: Routledge.
Wegerif, Rupert and Scrimshaw, Peter (eds) (1997) *Computers and talk in the primary classroom*. Clevedon: Multilingual Matters.
Wheeler, Tony *et al.* (1998) *101 easy-peasy things to do with your computer*. London: Kingfisher.

Websites: government

BECTA – *www.becta.org.uk* – The British Education and Communications Technology Agency website. It is concerned with all aspects of work with ICT in schools and contains many helpful links and resources on ICT research.
DfES – *www.dfes.gov.uk* – The Department for Education and Skills, including links through to DfES publications of various sorts.
DfES STANDARDS WEBSITE – *www.standards.dfes.gov.uk* – The Department for Education and Skills website which focuses on school achievement and performance and collects and presents huge numbers of statistics.
NATIONAL CURRICULUM IN ACTION – *www.ncaction.org.uk* – A government website which displays pupils' work showing attainment at different levels. This is very useful for developing an understanding of

progression and continuity in the various subject areas.

NATIONAL GRID FOR LEARNING – *www.ngfl.gov.uk* – The home page for the National Grid for Learning in the UK.

OFSTED – *www.ofsted.gov.uk* – The home page for the Inspection service, OFSTED, containing huge numbers of publications and reports.

TEACHER TRAINING AGENCY – *www.canteach.gov.uk* – The Teacher Training Agency (particularly useful for the latest information about the 'Skills tests' for QTS).

Websites: non-governmental

AMBLESIDE PRIMARY SCHOOL – *www.ambleside.schoolzone.co.uk* – Still the yardstick against which school websites try to measure themselves. Masses of resources and any number of brilliant ideas for how to use a school website. This goes way beyond the promotional material that some schools put on the Internet (the latest OFSTED, term dates etc.).

BOLTON ICT SUPPORT TEAM – *www.bgfl.org.uk* – An excellent example of local support for ICT in Schools.

BOOWAKWALA – *www.boowakwala.com* – Foundation Stage and Early Key Stage 1 resources.

EDUCATE THE CHILDREN – *www.educate.org.uk* – Accessible and usable resources in all subject areas.

GRID CLUB – *www.gridclub.com* – Secure online environment for schools.

HOW STUFF WORKS – *www.howstuffworks.com* – As described in the text. A wealth of user friendly information about computers and the Internet.

I LOVE LANGUAGES – *www.ilovelanguages.com* – A massive resource for multicultural education, including links to cultural websites, translation sites and more.

IDGBOOKS – *www.idgbooks.com* – Home of many computer guides for beginners.

MIRANDANET – *www.mirandanet.ac.uk* – Teachers, lecturers, ICT consultants and others exchange project ideas, and views on ICT in Education in a lively online forum.

MUSEUMS AND GALLERIES – *vlmp.museophile.com* – A comprehensive resource listing museum and gallery websites around the world.

NEWHAM ICT SUPPORT SERVICE – *itass.newham.gov.uk/curric* – Another excellent example of local support for ICT in Schools.

PRIMARY RESOURCES – *www.primaryresources.co.uk* – As described in the title…

TEACHING IDEAS – *www.teachingideas.co.uk* – As described in the title…

THINK – *www.think.com* – Oracle's excellent free online environment for education.

ULTRALAB – *www.ultralab.ac.uk* – ULTRALAB's website: inspiring ICT in Education projects.

Index